POWER AND MARGINALITY
IN CONTEMPORARY CAMEROONIAN ORATURE

Kansas City, MO (USA)

POWER AND MARGINALITY
IN CONTEMPORARY CAMEROONIAN ORATURE

Kashim Ibrahim Tala

**Power and Marginality
in Contemporary Cameroon Orature**
By Kashim Ibrahim Tala

First published 2013

Miraclaire Academic Publications (MAP)
8400 East 92nd Terrace, Kansas City, MO 64138, USA

Copyright © 2013 by Miraclaire Academic Publications

All rights for this book reserved.
No part of this book may be reproduced, stored in a retrieval system, or transmitted, in any form or by any means, electronic, mechanical, photocopying, recording or otherwise, without the prior permission of the copyright owner.

ISBN-13: 978-0615795782 / ISBN-10: 0615795781

Printed in the United States of America

MAP is an imprint of Miraclaire Publishing LLC
www.miraclairepublishing.com

Miraclaire Publishing makes every effort to ensure the accuracy of all the information ("Content") in its publications. However, Miraclaire and its agents and licensors make no representations or warranties whatsoever as to the accuracy, completeness, or suitability for any purpose of the Content and disclaim all such representations and warranties, whether expressed or implied to the maximum extent permitted by law. Any views expressed in this publication are the views of the author and are not necessarily the views of Miraclaire.

To Julie Enjema Tala

ACKNOWLEDGEMENTS

Most things in this world are accomplished by groups rather than by individuals working alone. This book is not an exception. Although I am personally responsible for the ideas in this book, many people provided me with assistance in the course of the project. Chief Nol Alembong, Dean of the Faculty of Arts, University of Buea, and Professor Shadrach Ambanasom, Deputy Director of the Higher Teachers Training College, University of Bamenda read through the manuscript painstakingly, and made helpful comments and criticisms.

My thanks are due to my young colleagues who provided me with intellectual support. They include Dr. Sone Enongene of the University of Swaziland, Dr. Niba Divine Che of the Ecole Normale Superieure, University of Yaounde 1, Dr. Gilead Ngam of the University of Bamenda, Dr. Nguefak Adeline of the University of Yaounde 1, and Dr. Ledoux Noel Fotio Jousse of the University of Dschang.

I would also like to thank my Ph.D students on whom I tested and tried out my ideas through lectures, discussions, and other academic platforms. Gilda Forbang, Fonge Theodore Esendege, Nchia Florence Mbi, Ahlijah Bernice Asi, Ayunnijam Rita Loumbunui, Otu George Ekpe, and Loninui Marie-Louise deserve special mention.

I also owe my family and friends a debt of gratitude for the socioemotional support they have provided me over the years. Lastly, I could not have completed this book without the love, care, and encouragement of my dear wife, Julie Enjema Tala. I remain forever in her debt.

FOREWORD

The function of the committed oral artist in Africa, in keeping with our traditions and societal needs, demands that he or she, as a public voice, assumes a responsibility to reflect public concerns in his or her artistic productions. The artist, in this connection, perceives social realities and makes those perceptions available in his or her art in order to help promote society's norms and values or bring pressure to bear on individuals and institutions. It is this commitment of the verbal artist and the relevance of orature to life that Kashim Ibrahim Tala focuses on in this seminal and timely book, *Power and Marginality in Contemporary Cameroonian Orature.*

Informed by ideas expressed in Cameroonian oral tales, proverbs and popular or protest songs, and based on some of the key tenets of New Historicism and Post-colonial theory, the author, in his analysis, seeks to answer questions that relate to the relationship between orature and contemporary life in Cameroon, the role orature plays in the socio-economic and politico-cultural development of Cameroon, the way verbal artists can change society for the better, the way the gap between the affluent centre and the indigent periphery can be bridged in an ever-changing Cameroon and, lastly, the way the balance of power in Cameroon can be off-set. These are pertinent issues that have not attracted much critical attention as far as scholarship on Cameroonian orature goes. The author has handled them with lucidity and insight from the position of a detached critic, an informed observer of society and a seasoned scholar.

Professor Nol Alembong,
Dean, Faculty of Arts,
University of Buea.

PREFACE

The idea of writing this book is derived from my long interest in the relationship between literature and politics. The treatment of political and social issues through the medium of orature has interested such humanistic or socio-scientific disciplines as sociology, anthropology, history, politics, literature, etc. But, scholars seem to have the predilection of approaching the study of power and marginality from the perspectives of the privileged minority who wield political and economic power. Very few scholars have taken the pains to address the subject from the viewpoint of the marginalized majority who have been distanced from the centre of power and who have become the unwitting victims of the rapacious use of power.

      This is where the significance of this book lies. It paints a rather sordid picture of the imbroglio in which postcolonial Cameroonians find themselves. That is, it highlights where Cameroonians have gone wrong, where the rain began to beat them. It then examines the roles of the different stakeholders in the game of political and economic power in Cameroon, and outlines what each of them can do to bridge the gap between those in positions of power and the ostracized majority. Put in slightly different terms, it underscores what can be done to restore a true sense of belonging to most Cameroonians, and what can be done to bring about some redress, reparation, indeed positive social, economic, and political change. It then brings to the fore, the didactic proportions of orature, and more importantly, how Cameroonians can benefit from their orature. It is from this standpoint that it posits that Cameroonian protest musicians are better placed to use their artistic skills to help in the daunting task of off-setting the balance of power in favour of the marginalized.

      The book has been designed to meet the needs of a variety of readers, whether general or academic.

Kashim Ibrahim TALA

Contents

ACKNOWLEDGEMENTS ...... *ii*
FOREWORD ...... *iii*
PREFACE ...... *iv*

INTRODUCTORY CONSIDERATIONS 1

CHAPTER ONE
LITERATURE AND SOCIETY 50

CHAPTER TWO
ORATURE AND ETHOLOGICAL EDUCATION 80

CHAPTER THREE
POPULAR SONGS AND PERCEPTIONS OF
NATIONHOOD 113

CHAPTER FOUR
THE POLITICAL ECONOMY OF DEPENDENCY 144

CHAPTER FIVE
THE WAY FORWARD 159

GENERAL CONCLUSION 189

BIBLIOGRAPHY 198

INTRODUCTORY CONSIDERATIONS

The centre, more or less visible, is the place from which power – political, military, economic, social, religious or ethical – emanates. At a second level, marginality thus becomes synonymous with the relative or absolute lack of power to influence a defined social entity while being a recipient of the exercise of power by other parts of that entity (Adebayo Adedeji).

Broad Strokes

This book examines the themes of "Power" and "Marginality" as they affect political governance in Cameroon and as they are reflected in contemporary Cameroonian orature. The focus is to demonstrate how Cameroonian orature can open a window of understanding into the current political process in Cameroon with a view to drawing implications for positive change. It is based on the following hypothetical contentions: Firstly, that far from being a static or an anachronistic literature as is perceived by some, orature is, in fact, a vibrant and dynamic literature which is shaped by social, political and economic forces in society. As a result, its life is closely tied to the life of the people. Secondly, that orature can play an important potential role in influencing society's perception and sense of direction. Thirdly, that Cameroonians cannot find their salvation in technological and scientific advances alone. They must be prepared to turn again to their culture and tradition. But, as Ali Mazrui (1986:20) warns,

> *Two broad principles should influence and inform social reform in Africa in the coming decades. One is the imperative of looking inwards towards ancestry; the other is the imperative of looking outward towards the wider humanity. The inward imperative requires a more systematic investigation into the cultural preconditions of the success of each project, of each piece of legislation, of each system of government. Feasibility studies should be much more sensitive to the issue of 'cultural feasibility' than has been the case in the past.*

> *Africa's ancestors need to be consulted through the intermediary of consulting African usage, custom and tradition.*

Finally, that for any meaningful change to occur, the impetus must come from within Cameroon and must be spearheaded by Cameroonians themselves. This book therefore sets out through an analysis of selected Cameroonian oral tales, proverbs and popular or protest songs to attempt answers to the following questions:

- What is the relationship between orature and contemporary life in Cameroon?
- What role can orature play in the socio-economic and politico-cultural development of Cameroon?
- How can the producers of orature use their skills to help change the future direction of society?
- How can the gap between the affluent centre and the indigent periphery be bridged in an ever-changing Cameroon?
- How can the balance of power in Cameroon be off-set in favour of the exploited and oppressed majority?

Definition of Terms

The arguments raised in this volume revolve around certain key terms and concepts which require that I should define and situate them within the context in which I intend to use them. They are "power", "marginality", "Cameroon", and "orature". I will also provide contextual definitions for such fundamental terms as "neo-colonialism" and "globalization". I will begin with "orature" since it is the raw material of this book. Early European scholars of African orature subsumed it under "folklore" perhaps because folklore encompasses the collective heritage of a rustic people, and also because it lends credence to the Eurocentric view that African culture is still in its primitive stages. Consequently, it may be necessary for me to begin by answering the question, what is folklore? Since there is no consensus of opinion as to the meaning of that term, I am of the opinion that three definitions by professional folklorists will provide sufficient cognitive, expressive and social distinctive features of folklore for the purposes of this study. According to Jan Harold Bruvand (1978:2-3),

> *Folklore is the traditional, unofficial, non-institutional part of culture. It encompasses all knowledge, understanding, values, attitudes, assumptions, feelings, and beliefs transmitted in traditional forms by word of mouth or by customary examples. Many of these habits of thought are common to all human beings, but they always interact with and are influenced by the whole cultural context that surrounds them. Folklore manifests itself in many oral and verbal forms (mentifacts), in kinesiological forms (customary behavior or sociofacts), and in material forms (artifacts), but folklore itself is the whole traditional complex of thought, content, and process which ultimately can never be fixed or recorded in its entirety; it lives only in performance or communication as people interact with one another.*

For Bruvand, folklore is a collective term for the valuable heritage of indigenous people which is transmitted orally, by imitation, and by other means. It is a compendium of the genius of a people and therefore a living phenomenon. Bruvand goes further to reduce the diverse materials and manifestations of folklore into three convenient groups: what people say (verbal folklore), what people do (customary folklore), and what people make (material folklore). What Bruvand designates as "verbal folklore," is what I refer to in this book as orature.

William Bascom (1953:283), on his part, lays emphasis on Bruvand's first sub-category which is, "what people say". That explains why he sees folklore from a narrower perspective as "a part of culture, but not the whole of culture. It includes myths, legends, tales, proverbs, riddles, the texts of ballads and other songs". All the forms listed by Bascom, as I will demonstrate later on, are incorporated under the term "orature". Finally, Dan Ben Amos (in Lindfors 1977:1-2) adopts the general definition of folklore advanced by Bruvand. But, like Bascom, his emphasis is on the verbal lore of the people. However, he goes beyond Bascom to comment on the functional aspects of the lore of the people and the social context of performance.

> The forms of folklore as speakers delineate and recognize them have cultural and symbolic meanings. Texts, framed into genres and performed in socially defined communicative situations, acquire significances beyond the literal meanings of their constituent words. Ritual songs, for example, which abound with repetitions and obscure terms, are rendered meaningless outside their verbal or social contexts; or, in other cases, their transition from one context to another involves a transformation of meaning. Genealogies and legends function towards the promotion of social stability because they are symbolic expressions of political power and historical truth; parables are effective in settling personal disputes due to their capacity to symbolize moral truth, and tales and riddles can entertain because of their inherent ability to unsettle reality.

The definition of folklore given by Dan Ben Amos touches on some key features of orature. For example, he sees folklore as folk literature which is socially conditioned, which is secular in intent and which performs social, political and economic functions.

Thus, it is this association of orature with folklore which has led some well-meaning but misdirected literary scholars to refuse to ascribe the status of literature to orature. Fortunately, the situation is changing very fast.

Still, I am yet to answer the question, what is orature? However, to answer this question, I will have to first answer another question, what is literature? This exercise is necessary because, as I intend to demonstrate, orature is literature in its own right albeit with its own specialist terminologies and approaches.

Generally, literature is described as a work of art expressed in carefully selected language (spoken or written) which deals with the thoughts, concepts and ideas of an individual or a people. In other words, it is the creative production of the human mind couched in figurative language. For example, when an individual expresses his joys or sorrows through language effectively, literature can be said to be in the making. Hence, when a literary piece has been composed orally, performed orally, is transmitted orally, and is presented in a special literary language, it is considered orature. The Cameroonians who produce and use orature perceive it as secular in intent and serving political, economic and social functions. As Richard Olaniyan (1982:1) has observed,

> *The peoples of Africa, like all other peoples of the world, are inseparable from their history and culture, for their history is the record of what they did, thought and said; and their culture is the totality of the ideas, concepts and values that characterize their societies. These cultural elements are manifested in their literatures (oral as well as written), religions, social, economic and political institutions, music and dance, arts and drama, and their languages – all these in turn have been and still are profoundly influenced by their environments.*

Harold Courlander (1975:1) posits that orature in the past as in the present derived and continues to derive its raw material from the realities of society and is used by the people to articulate their worldview and to examine individual experience in relation to the normative order of society:

> *Man in Africa, as elsewhere, has sought to relate his past to his present, and to tentatively explore the future so that he might not stand lonely and isolated in the great sweep of time, or intimidated by the formidable earth and the vast stretch of surrounding seas. In his myths and legends he bridges back to the very dream morning of creation, while in his systems of divination he projects himself into time not yet come; in his epics he asserts the courage and worth of human species; in his tales he ponders on what is just or unjust, upon what is feeble or courageous, what is sensible or ridiculous, or what moves the spirit to grief or to exultation; in his proverbs and sayings he capsulates the learnings of centuries about the human character and about the intricate balance between people and the world around them.*

Apart from helping man to make sense of his relationship with his environment, orature also performs several functions in society. As Olaniyan (175) points out,

> Literature is a work of art expressed in words to mirror life and to be perceived intellectually to uplift the mind and the soul. As a work of art, it has aesthetic value for man, exuding beauty and thereby giving him satisfaction and pleasure. As a mirror to life, it instructs man in the ways of the world, making life more intelligible to him. As an intellectual exercise, it uplifts the mind and the soul of man, showing him how to live better, die better and leave the world a better place. Finally being all three things (a work of art, a mirror to life and an intellectual exercise) rolled into an indivisible whole expressed in words, literature has humanizing, unifying, consolidating and even revolutionizing effects on man and society.

Edgar V. Roberts and Henry E. Jacobs (2000:1) assert that literature helps to increase the range of our experience and provide references for cultural practice:

> Literature helps us grow both personally and intellectually. It opens the cultural, philosophical and religious practices of which we are part. It enables us to recognize human dreams and struggles in different places and times that we otherwise would never know existed. It gives us the knowledge and perception to appreciate the beauty of order and arrangement. It provides the comparative basis from which to see worthiness in the aims of all peoples.

It is this intricate relationship between literature and society that has generated renewed interest in the study of orature in Cameroon today. As Paul Mbangwana (1993:250) has remarked,

> Our traditional and cultural heritage is so clear to us because it protects our customs, beliefs and worldviews. This heritage is relevant to us because our contemporary problems are better solved within the perspectives of such old cultural patterns. It is necessary to reason and reflect upon these time-honoured values for inspiration and guidance.

The characteristic ambivalence of African orature is responsible for the inability of scholars to evolve an appropriate taxonomy. This impasse, as Ademola Dasylva (1999:2) asserts, is further complicated by the fact that

> Each major cultural group in Africa has its peculiarities and cultural idiosyncrasy which determine the form, structure and scope of its oral traditions. Some of these peculiarities are often unlikely to be common to most other cultural regions. Therefore they tend to make any attempt at regimentation, classification and generalization (at generic, characterologic and syntagmatic levels) of oral literary forms problematic.

It is not my intention to continue the debate here. As a result, the terms that I am using in this book to describe the different genres of orature are the same as those used in Western literary study because they are widely recognized and the reader is likely to be familiar with them. That explains why the principal oral genres studied in this book are identified as oral tales, proverbs, and popular songs. It also explains why I am using the terms orature and oral literature interchangeably.

The Oral Tale

The oral tale is, perhaps, the most popular form of orature in Cameroon. It is usually the first genre to be discovered by students of orature. It is also the only form on which so much has been written over the years. According to Stith Thompson (1977:4), the oral tale is employed in much broader sense to include all forms of prose narrative, written or oral, which have come to be handed down through the years. In this usage, the important fact is the traditional nature of the material. In contrast to the modern storywriter's striving after originality of plot and treatment, the teller of a folktale is proud to hand on that which he has received.

To the Nigerian oralist, Helen Chukwuma (1981:12), on the other hand,

> The oral tale is the traditional folktale. Its characteristics are brevity, terseness, episodic plot and action, climactic heightening of a central conflict and

> the limitation of character. The oral tale...portrays an aspect of life and reality through varied means. The final goal is to bring to man a knowledge and awareness of his nature and environment... The oral tale is a child of tradition, almost always apocryphal, belonging to the whole community. It enjoys abundant freedom and identifies with anyone in the community who can articulate it creditably. Plagiarism makes no sense with regards to the oral tale, and for its purposes, the important feature is the performer and not the coiner.

Finally, Peter Seitel (1980:30) defines oral tales as,

> Metaphors for aspects of social life. They are abstract, artistic statements that objectify and grant perspective on the culture they describe. They enable Hayas to hold aspects of their social world at arm's length, so to speak, to examine them, and to entertain themselves with those images of their own lives.

From the definitions of the oral tale given above, it can be said that the oral tale is by its very nature short. It restricts its focus to a narrow bit of experience, it avoids digressions from its main intentions, it utilizes easily recognizable characters, and it emphasizes the moral lessons inherent in the outcome of the actions of the fictive character. In other words, the oral tale focuses on the dynamics of relations between the individual and society. That explains why the characters in the oral tale are deliberately undeveloped and why almost anything can be a character in the oral tale.

Proverbs

Proverbs are a dynamic literary genre in Cameroon. They are also important aspects of style in the sense that they represent some homely truths expressed in a concise manner. Proverbs are generally framed around a central image which reflects aspects of life. As Bascom (478) observes, "the fact that the proverbs express moral and value judgments indicating what is right or wrong and what is good or bad gives them an important place in African ethical teachings".

Ojo Arewa and Alan Dundes (1964: 74) on their part, assert that,

> *In any society where man interacts with his fellow men, the correct procedure for that interaction is usually outlined. And the nature of this interaction, at least in terms of ideal culture, is more often than not communicated to the members by the instrumentality of proverbs.*

The point made by Arewa and Dundes explains why proverbs are protected by traditional sanctions and why they offer immunity from censure to their users. It is also from this perspective that Heda Jason (197: 617) sees the proverb as a very convenient vehicle because "all the connotations of a traditional expression are well known and the risk of being misunderstood is reduced. Still more important is the circumstance that the opinions expressed by the proverb, the message it carries, are traditionally sanctioned from public censure".

Finally, Olowo Ojoade (in Ongoum and Tcheho, 1985:100) posits that,

> *No serious scholar of the proverb can fail to notice that the proverb is commonly utilized to reprove any member of the society who misbehaves, to praise or censure, to give support or to withdraw support from a venture and to indoctrinate members concerning the acceptable standard of social behavior.*

For the purposes of this study then, I shall simply define proverbs as popular sayings that carry authority. They are circulated orally and are marked by the didacticism of the content and the conciseness of form. They originate from everyday activities and embrace the philosophical and socio-cultural value systems of the people. They are also universal in their occurrences, sources and characteristics. Viewed in this light, the proverb, like the oral tale is an important mechanism for maintaining the stability of culture, for molding public opinion and for inculcating ethical standards in the young.

The Folk Song

Of the three oral genres under study, the folk song, otherwise known as oral poetry, is by far the most popular in Cameroon. It is generally defined as a short lyric text which is set to music and which appeals to a wide range of people. It is an integral part of the Cameroonian heritage and contributes to ceremonial and festival occasions. It is spontaneous and takes the whole of the people's experience as its subject matter. It is performed generally for the artistic gratification of the folk singer and his audience in a restricted context. According to Bole Butake (in Tala, 1999:44),

> *The song or poem is the most basic and profuse form of emotive expression in African societies. The African manifests his feelings through an outburst of song when he loves and when he hates, when he works and when he plays, when he is at peace and when he fights, when a child is born and when death takes its toll. The song then is the lifeline of the African; and he learns the art of poetry because he is born and bred in a society which recognizes that the poetic form is, emotionally, most expressive of the human predicament.*

Folksongs are functional in the sense that some of them are didactic in content. That is, they emphasize the correct and acceptable moral conduct of the society and are intended to have a positive moral influence on the community. In other words, they exert a strong moral force and are often used didactically and as social correctives. As J.L. Campton (1981:310) puts it,

> *A folk song is usually a medium for group communication which serves to bring the attention of groups to a common focus, to prepare them for a singular response, and to produce consensus. Song texts usually focus on those problems, interests, and concerns common to a large segment of the community. If this is not so, a folk song will not likely hold the audience's attention and its transmission into oral tradition will probably not take place. As a result, the text of folk songs is generally loaded with normative subject matter.*

Ruth Finnegan (1970:82) also commented on the close relationship between orature, politics and the traditional African state. According to her,

> *The patronage of poets in centralized political systems in the past led to the creation of a poetry of profound*

political significance as a means of political propaganda, pressure or communication; such poetry includes insult, challenge or satirical comment used as politically effective weapons.

Thus, even in traditional African society, the folk song was used as a powerful vehicle of social and political ideas. As Kofi Agovi (1995:48) explains, "The politicization of literature in African society was inevitable because literature, or artistic forms, became the nerve centre of a network of complementary institutions which were integrated into the state machinery by virtue of their pursuit of similar or related goals and ideals".

The Popular Song
Popular songs evolved from folk songs and continued with the treatment of themes of immediate political and social significance. The artists also followed in the footsteps of their ancestors in traditional African societies and continued to criticize and evaluate the political leadership in order to determine the extent to which it promotes the people's desire for stability, peace, and meaningful development. The only difference then, is the addition of the term "popular" to the new songs. According to Bertolt Brecht (in Gugelberger, 1985:10) "popular" means:

Intelligible to the broad masses, adopting and enriching their forms of expression/ assuming their standpoint, confirming and correcting it/ representing the most progressive section of the people so that it can assume leadership, and therefore intelligible to other sections of the people as well/ relating to traditions and developing them/ communicating to that portion of the people which strives for leadership the achievement of the section that at present rules the nation.

The term "popular song" has therefore been used here to refer also to protest songs. In other words, "popular" and "protest" will be used in this book to refer to the same phenomenon. That is, a song composed and sung by the people to criticize and evaluate the political process. J. Street (2001:254) also emphasizes the political functions of popular songs or protest music especially their use to comment on power, question and, in some cases, even contest power.

> *Music does not exist autonomously of other social, economic and political institutions. Music may still be able to change the world as well as reflecting it, but, when we talk of music's politics, we are not just talking of the way it articulates ideas and emotions. We are talking of the politics that shape it.*

Cameroon has in the last fifty years produced an impressive panoply of popular musicians, prominent among whom are Manu Dibango, Francis Bebey, Anne Marie Nzie, Tala Andre Marie, Lapiro de Mbanga, Petit Pays, Longue Longue, Douleur, Prince Yerima Afo Akom, Sergio Polo, Prince Nico Mbarga, Ndedi Eyango, and Sally Nyolo. These Musicians have won great renown both nationally and internationally. Thanks to their creativity and innovation, Cameroon can occupy the same pedestal as the Democratic Republic of Congo, Cote d'Ivoire, and Nigeria as distinguished centres for the production and consumption of popular music in Africa.

Cameroonian musicians have also produced varied local genres of popular music which reflect the country's cultural diversity and ethnicity. For example, there is the Makossa from the Littoral, Bikutsi from the Centre, Bend Skin and Mangambeau from the West, and Njang and Bottle Dance from the North West.

The themes of the songs are varied and cover such key areas as politics, economics, culture, and gender. For instance, the politically inclined songs fall into two broad groups: those which serve the interests of the politicians and those which openly challenge the status quo. The latter group of popular songs inveigh against the rapacious use of power and the endemic economic crises in the country. They denounce social injustices especially the tendency of the people in positions of power to forget the people they govern. They indict the educated elite for their collusion with corrupt political officials and their own involvement with corruption; and they also condemn the unbridled materialism of the society.

The importance of popular songs as powerful and flexible vehicle for political communication has been substantially enhanced by their incorporation within the matrix of popular music which is a hybrid of western instrumentation and local rhythms and lyrics. Through their music, the artists reach out to a broad audience at all levels of the society. But, those who actually patronize the protest music more are those in the lower economic scale. That is, the unemployed youth and other underprivileged members of the society perhaps because they are the ones who bear the brunt of the socio-economic and political injustices in the country. The wide reach and particularly the grassroots appeal of the protest music make it an open platform for the understanding of everyday experience and a powerful medium of political activism.

But, the ascendancy of the popular song on the Cameroonian musical scene came with its own set of peculiar problems and also introduced new production, distribution and commercialization relations in the life of Cameroonians. To begin with, there is no consistent and appropriate cultural policy in Cameroon. There is no capacity building strategy for both artists and trainers. That is, there is no school or training centre in Cameroon for the formal education of popular artists and their trainers. As a result, anybody aspiring to this relatively new profession has no alternative but to revert to the traditional system of education. That is, by individual contact through watching and imitating the experts. In fact, virtually all the established Cameroonian popular artists were inducted into music in that way. Furthermore, in the past, traditional music was performed mainly for the aesthetic gratification of the artist and his audience; and the fame of the artist rested on the artistic merit of his performance. Now, all that has changed. The popular song has become a commodity which is subject to the exigencies of the market. The venue for broadcasting popular songs has shifted from the public arena to professional recording studios. That has necessitated a change in the production techniques. For instance, the popular artist is now obliged to use the ancillary services of professionals who write, record, edit, manufacture, distribute and market the songs. To complicate matters, the production of a musical album requires heavy financial investment. And since most of the Cameroonian artists cannot afford the high cost of production, they are obliged to depend on financial assistance from rich sponsors. Similarly, Cameroon has no firm legal, regulatory framework which can protect the artists from exploitation by fraudulent middlemen. Finally, Cameroon has no official strategy for ensuring the enforcement of Intellectual Property and Copyright Laws. This subordination of popular songs to the forces of the market especially those of supply and demand has the potential of eroding the autonomy of the popular artists. As the Mexican Marxist aesthetician, Adolfo Sanchez Vazquez (1973:84) opines,

> *In capitalist society, a work of art is 'productive' when it is market oriented, when it submits itself to the exigencies of the market, the fluctuations of supply and demand. And since there is no objective measure by which to determine the value of his particular merchandise, the artist is subject to the tastes, preferences, ideas, and aesthetic notions of those who influence the market. Inasmuch as he produces works of art destined for a market that absorbs them, the artist cannot fail to heed the exigencies of this market: they often affect the content as well as the form of a work of art, thus placing limitations on the artist, stifling his creative potential, his individuality.*

Thus, the Cameroonian artists, unlike their counterparts elsewhere, are operating against all odds. They also have to contend with the heavy hand of a government which is allergic to criticism. Nevertheless, the fact remains that the Cameroonian protest musicians have come down on the side of the ordinary people against their oppressors. Their commitment to the cause of the ordinary people have put them on the firing line in their opposition to the political forces whom they see as betraying the people in whose name independence was won. Hence, Cameroon popular music continues to be intensely political and there is every indication that it is destined to remain so for quite some time. The artists are in the thick of the fight for the true liberation of their people, a position which is still fraught with dangers.

From their understanding and interpretation of the Cameroonian political scene, the Cameroonian popular artists whose songs have been selected for study in this book can be considered as democratic agents who see themselves as part of the suffering masses. That is why they create their songs for the good of the society. If they are concerned in their songs with issues of good governance, freedom of expression and accountability, it is because they believe in the primacy of public interest over the selfish interests of some spineless political officials. It is also because they believe that good governance should be interpreted to mean the orderly organization of government so that it can respond effectively to the aspirations of the suppressed and exploited masses. Thus, the main concern of the artists is to help their people to have a clear idea of what a well organized government is all about, and an understanding of what constitutes their collective aspirations. In other words, they use their songs to conscientize their people. The term "conscientization" has been used here in the same sense in which Shadrach Ambanasom (2003: 124-125) has used it:

> *Conscientization implies the education of the masses, especially the oppressed masses, in such a way that they become imbued with a heightened sense of critical consciousness. When oppressed people become conscientized, they tend to know more about certain issues and situations than they did before. They become more familiar with the inner structure of their society and the dynamics of the vicious system that has held them captives.*

In approaching the core issues of this book, I have taken into consideration the fact that there are major shifts that are discernible in the overall landscape of Cameroonian orature. These fall into several inter-related areas. For example, there is the gradual transfer of the setting from the rural to the urban areas; the widening of the thematic content to reflect the important issues of today; the transformation of the role of the oral artist into an acerbic and virulent political critic, and the intricate relationship that now exists between orature and politics in Cameroon and elsewhere. I have also acknowledged the fact that some genres of Cameroonian orature are losing their relative popularity. But, I consider that as only natural. For when some forms lose their popularity, other forms are likely to gain it. For instance, the oral tale is fast ceding its prominent place in the hierarchy of genres to the popular song which now constitute the crux of urban orature. Liz Gunner (in Ngeh, 2011: 200), reinforces this point when she said that:

> *In an era of globalization, orality has not disappeared but has often adapted itself in its many different forms to become a vehicle for the expression of the fears and hopes of new generations of Africans. Thus while it is true that, in some instances, genres of poetry or song and narrative have not endured the erosion of the social base that sustained their performances and their producers, other genres have survived or grown.*

Thus, while some genres are losing their prominence, all the genres of Cameroonian orature are, in their own way, adapting to the intense social and political change which Cameroon is undergoing. The oral texts selected for study in this book are acts of communication and defiance between the majority who are marginal in the power structure of Cameroon and the minority who hold and exercise absolute power. In other words, the texts emanate from the periphery to contest the dominant ideology of the centre. Seen from this perspective, the texts constitute a counter-power. That is, power exercised by the weak upon those who are stronger. The implication here is that the weak and dispossessed are not entirely helpless. They can, if they really want to, acquire a significant degree of agency by means of their resilience in the face of oppression and exploitation.

I will now focus on "Cameroon" which is the geographical context in which this study evolves. The nation which we call Cameroon today had its origin in the territorial demarcation drawn by the German, French, and British colonial powers following undefined geostrategic considerations and regardless of ethnic, cultural, or religious considerations. In order to justify their imperial expansion, the colonial authorities deliberately denigrated indigenous Cameroonian cultures. That sparked off a war of cultures in which the indigenous cultures suffered. The relegation of local cultures to the margins meant that Cameroonians were no longer at ease under the dominant European culture.

The colonial authorities further super-imposed their economic, political and educational institutions on Cameroon as part of the colonial process. But these institutions never took root in the country because they were shallow, weak, and undeveloped. The main reason for that was the fact that the colonial administration did not have the goodwill and, therefore, did very little to help Cameroon to strengthen its institutions, especially those that promote democracy and accountability. That was ironical because it was the very colonial administration which emphasized democracy and accountability as the way forward for Cameroon.

The colonial administration also propagated the politics of regional and ethnic balance and, before long, Cameroon became a fertile ground for foundationary binary inscriptions such as the centre and the margin, the rich and the poor, the privileged and the under-privileged, the haves and the have nots, the them and the us. Thus, under the colonial dispensations, Cameroonians could not develop a common sense of belonging and purpose. Hence the allegiance and loyalty of a Cameroonian was more to his family than to an amorphous and artificial national entity. To complicate matters, the rootlessness and illegitimacy of the colonial administration, as I will demonstrate later, facilitated the institutionalization of bribery and corruption as a way of life by the high and low of the country. In conclusion, it can be said that colonialism helped to widen rather than bridge the gap between the centre and the margin in Cameroon. As a consequence of colonialism, Cameroonians have been constrained to become men and women of two worlds and are having difficulties in reconciling the Cameroonian and European elements of their personality. Bernth Lindfors (in Olaniyan, 2008:25), describes the dilemma of Africans including Cameroonians as follows:

> *Either things fell apart in the village or people fell apart in the cities. In both cases Africa was no longer at ease because a collision with Europe had knocked it off*

> *balance. The legacy of colonialism was cultural confusion, and it was virtually impossible to find stable moral values in societies or individuals mired in such a mess. Contrary to Western colonial mythology, Europe did not bring light, peace and justice to the Dark Continent; it brought chaos to what has once been a well-ordered world.*

In spite of the negative impact of colonialism on Cameroonians, however, the people still attempted to see themselves as belonging to a nation, at least in principle. That is, as sharing a common history, dreams and aspirations. But, the fact remains that Cameroon under colonial rule, remained, in reality, a fragmented nation in search of unity and cohesion.

Political independence when it finally came, accelerated the degenerative process started by colonialism. Those who inherited the new Cameroonian nation were quick to abdicate their primary responsibility of laying concrete foundation for post-colonial development and progress. The people in power used their positions to enrich themselves at the expense of the masses, while the masses, unable to understand what was happening to them, looked on in utter bewilderment. Thus, it is the materialistic individualism of the political leadership, the rapaciousness with which the elite pursue wealth, and the general apathy of the people that exacerbated the economic and political woes of post-colonial Cameroon and prompted the intervention of the protest musicians.

In the light of the above, Cameroonian protest musicians identify four basic factors as responsible for the deplorable state of affairs and the resultant tensions in contemporary Cameroon. These factors as the selected songs under study indicate are the unbridled materialism of the society, the general lack of a sense of national unity and national integration, society's cynicism and apathy, and the lack of political vision and sense of direction on the part of the leaders.

The protest musicians want to transform Cameroon into a country in which sharing, justice, peace, and freedom prevail. That is why they use their songs to open a dialogue between the centre and the margins, to break away from imprisoning binaries and to forge a convergence of the two opposing forces in order to ensure progress and development. Thus, the protest musicians though disenchanted, disillusioned and seething with anger at what Cameroonians are making of their political inheritance, they do not despair. They believe that Cameroon has great potentials for the future. That is why they are using their songs to castigate the institutions of their country in the hope of bringing about desirable changes. Their songs cover the past, the present, and predict the future of Cameroon because they hold the view that the past informs the present and is determinant of the future. In other words, the problems of contemporary Cameroon cannot be solved without recourse to the lessons and wisdom of the past.

My use of the blanket term "Cameroon" to cover a study of a handful of oral genres may appear at first sight to be preposterous. But, when looked at more closely, it is, in fact, appropriate. There is no doubt that Cameroon is one of the most culturally, linguistically, socially and politically diverse countries in Africa with each major cultural group having its peculiarities and idiosyncrasies which determine the form, structure and scope of its orature. But, Cameroonians also share several things in common. They share a tenuous sense of nationhood. They are among the most economically exploited people in the world. They are also among the most backward in terms of industrial development, global commerce, and access to information and communication technologies. It is therefore clear from what has gone before that the issues raised in the oral texts selected for study in this book about Power and Marginality and about political, economic, and social instability affect most Cameroonians.

Power
Having defined the immediate socio-political and cultural context of the work, I will now direct my attention to the next key concept which is, "power". Much of what I will be saying in this book has its roots in issues related to power. It will be recalled that power has been a key consideration among people and cultures for a long time. People in power have also been

known to employ guns, money and even histrionics as devices for gaining and retaining power over others.

The question that comes to mind here is: what is power? The answer to this question can be found in the very definition of the term. However, there is no consensus as to what power really is. In other words, power is an umbrella word which means different things to different people in different cultures. Therefore, I will limit myself to those definitions of the term which I consider to be closest to the concerns of this book. Kent L. Sandstrom (2003:140) for example, suggests that "power is the capacity to get other people to think, feel, or act the way you want them to even if they do not want to think, feel, or act this way". W. Buckley (1967:186), on his part, defines power as "control or influence over the actions of others to promote one's goals without their consent, against their will, or without their knowledge or understanding." Finally, S. Nanda and R.L. Warms (1998:226) tell us that "power is the ability to make and carry out decisions affecting one's own life, control the behavior of other human beings, and transform objects and resources". It can therefore be deduced from the three definitions given above that what makes power an important dimension in society and, consequently, a potential problem is that power usually means controlling your own life and the lives of others.

What is significant about power is that its methods are as diverse as they are widespread. That is to say that power is ubiquitous from national and international politics to face-to-face interactions between those who have power and those who do not have. The implication here is that in a power relationship there is an interaction between two parties, the power holder and the target person in which the behavior of the target person is controlled by the power holder. This presupposes that power results from unequal dependency. That is, one party in a relationship possesses what the other party needs but does not have. As a consequence of this disequilibrium, the target party becomes more dependent on the power holder and is subject to his control. Put differently, the people in power tend to have a major impact on what other people believe and do, and they also invariably influence the rules of appropriate and inappropriate behavior. Thus, although all men are supposedly born equal, some men are obviously more equal than others. Hence, I intend in this book to use the term "power" to mean the capacity of the minority in authority to influence and control the majority whom they rule.

Dependency, as I will demonstrate later on in this book, is a key factor in many relationships. In the Cameroonian context, for example, I shall look at power relationships within Cameroon and power relationships between Cameroon and other nations. In some power relationships, parties interact as equals and have about the same amount of power. But, in the kind of power relationships that I will be dealing with in this book, parties interact on an unequal basis. In other words, one party possesses more power than the other party because of the status it occupies.

Marginality
The party that possesses less power is considered to be on the margin. That is, far away from the centre of power. Graham Furniss and Liz Gunner (1995: xii) see "Marginality" within the context of particular power relations as the "differential positions between social categories, for example, men and women or between the old and the young, and to social distance from a seat of constituted power within a particular society". Thus, "Marginality" exists within unequal power relations and constitutes one of the basic characteristics of asymmetrical relationships. For Sandstrom (139),

> *A relationship is asymmetrical when one of its participants establishes control or dominance, disproportionately imposing his or her will on the other participants and setting conditions, making decisions, and engaging in actions that determine the form and course of the relationship.*

It is this form of asymmetrical relationship which exists between Cameroonians who belong to the superordinate group and those who belong to the subordinate group within the country, and the economically powerless Cameroon and the economically powerful countries of the North that the oral texts under study decry. Asymmetrical relationships are usually caused by wanton abuse of power and inevitably lead to the marginalization of the less powerful group by the more powerful. Seen from this perspective, the marginalized group is likely to cry foul and take the action necessary to redress the situation. This raises the question, what can be done to redress the situation? One medium which is at the disposal of the oppressed and dispossessed group and which does not require the use of physical violence is orature. It has been used in the past to comment on power relations in society and to bring benevolent dictators to their knees. I am convinced that if properly appreciated and fully exploited, it can be used again today to raise the level of consciousness in society thereby provoking positive change. In other words, orature can reflect and affect social and political life in contemporary Cameroon. Seen in this light, it is a significant agent of change and can be used to overeturn and recast perceptions of social reality. In fact this is the use to which the protest musicians have put their songs. Thus, I have deliberately chosen the two words "Power" and "Marginality" as key concepts in the title of this book because they aptly describe the two ends of the spectrum of power relations that I will be dealing with.

In order to better appreciate the complexity of the other two fundamental terms, "neo-colonialism" and "globalization" as used in the context of this study, it is necessary to go down the historical lane to the attainment of political independence by Cameroonians in particular and Africans in general.

Political independence implies the making of something modern and democratic out of the existing social structure. It also means interdependence. That is a symbiotic relationship between two or more nations based on the principles of equality and reciprocity. The issue of interdependence is crucial here because, on the one hand, Cameroonians are obliged to live in a social context in which the action or inaction of an individual or groups of individuals affect others either positively or negatively. On the other hand, Cameroon as a nation is also obliged to live and cooperate with other nations in a world in which every people share a common humanity.

Therefore, interdependence, in the sense in which it is used here, is the direct opposite of dependency.

The attainment of political independence by many African countries including Cameroon in the sixties raised very high hopes and expectations. As the pioneer Cameroon Anglophone novelist, Mbella Sone Dipoko (in Gugelberger, 1985:29) points out,

> For the masses, happiness was, as is still is, a prospective dream. Better conditions of living, higher purchasing power, personal freedom, a share of all the good things of modern life, from industrial products to learning; in short, a longing for better days to come. The prestige which educated Africans have among their people shows how forward-looking the common man is...

But in the end independence did not bring significant positive change in the lives of the people. In place of life more abundant as promised by the politicians, the masses reaped suffering in abundance. Thus, to the innocent eye of the pre-independence era, the political activists or nationalists as they are better known, seemed the only hope in the social, economic and political struggle for the liberation of the beleaguered continent. They formed the only really vocal group of any size that showed signs of vitality and talked what sounded like a revolutionary language. Nationalist political parties were the only movements that claimed they would change the social and political structure in order to eliminate some, if not all the evils colonialism inflicted on society. But, when the struggle for political independence was accomplished, when the political parties were in power, the common man saw a reality that mocked his vision of a better society. He found himself in a society riddled with political ineptitude, ethnic bigotry, rising unemployment, galloping inflation, unbridled materialism, pervasive corruption and the failure of those who inherited power at independence to relate to the very people who legitimize their authority. To complicate matters, some democratically elected Cameroonian leaders tended to collude with the erstwhile colonial masters to milk the young nation dry. The venerable Cameroonian Professor, Bernard Nsokika

Fonlon in his seminal book, *To Every African Freshman* (1969:1) writes:

> Independence seems to have been won, but before long it is dawning upon us that what we have won is the shadow and not the reality of self-rule. For, from being slaves of our former masters, we have only been promoted to the dubious dignity of a beggar at his gate. We depend on him too much for the barest needs of life and beggars do not have the liberty to choose.

Fonlon is saying here that independence might have set Cameroonians free in a narrow political sense. But they are definitely not free economically and therefore cannot effectively chart their own destinies. The rather gloomy picture of post-independence Africa painted by Fonlon attests to the fact that political independence, as far as African countries including Cameroon are concerned was, in essence, without any tangible substance. But Lenin (in Gugelberger ,130) had foreseen that long ago and had warned that

> Precisely because the struggle for national liberation was led by the national bourgeoisie, the independent states that would emerge and that would typify the present historical stage would be states which while officially being politically independent would nevertheless, in fact remain enmeshed in the net of financial and diplomatic dependence on imperialism.
>
> ...by virtue of the class character of the national bourgeoisie of the oppressed nations, a situation would be brought about whereby a certain rapprochement would be arrived at so that even where the bourgeoisie of the oppressed countries does not support the national movement, it at the same time works hand in glove with the imperialist bourgeoisie, that is, joins forces with it against all revolutionary movements and revolutionary classes.

In the light of the above, Lenin observed that in the so-called independent countries while "the bourgeoisie of the oppressed nations merely talks about national revolt, in actual practice it enters into reactionary agreements with the bourgeoisie of the oppressing nations behind the backs of and against its own people" (130).

Scholars, thinkers, and artists in Africa and elsewhere have advanced several reasons for the bastardization of the political legacy which has occurred in Africa. One reason is that the African politicians who inherited political power from the erstwhile colonial masters were not prepared for the takeover. Another reason is the absence of legal and ethical precedents and ground rules on which the people themselves could assess and sanction their leaders. Yet another reason is the prevalence of political "godfatherism," a practice which allowed a relatively few smart opportunists to monopolize the positions of power in the government. But the most pertinent reason, as far as the prime theme of this book is concerned, is the one advanced by the eminent Nigerian writer, Chinua Achebe in (Umelo Ojinmah, 1991: 94). According to him, "power, whether political or religious, derives from the people and that its possessors should be accountable to the people". He goes further to attribute many of the excesses of post-independence African politicians to their ignoring of this fact. The answers to the question, what can Cameroon do to live up to the promise of its postcolonial dream will be given in subsequent chapters.

The personalization and monopolization of power in Cameroon has placed the state in the hands of a powerful minority thereby pushing 80 per cent of the population to the margin. It is this marginalization of the powerless majority more than anything else that has distanced Cameroon from global commerce and transformed it into a marionette in the hands of powerful multinational corporations like A.E.S. Sonel, Total, Orange and M.T.N. In so doing, it has also surreptitiously ushered into the country the hydra-headed monster of neo-colonialism otherwise known as long-distance economic domination. As G.E. Okereke in (Ngeh, 249) laments:

> *The African predicament is compounded by the re-emergence of colonialism in new robes bearing a slightly different name: neo-colonialism. This is a new kind of colonialism because Europe is now controlling Africa not directly as in the colonial era but indirectly through the African leaders.*

This colonialism by remote control may be relatively new in Africa but it is not a recent phenomenon in the world. In fact, it is an age- old insidious and invidious economic system used by the strong and powerful nations to keep the weak and powerless nations in perpetual economic bondage. As Harry Laidler in (Ngeh: 225) describes it:

> For thousands of years, those in control of political and industrial power in the nations of the world used that power to oppress the weak. For thousands of years, under every kind of industrial society, the great mass of world's burden bearers were doomed to lives of poverty and want, while the few lived in luxury. The few declared the wars; the many went forth to battle and to death. The few made the laws, told the many under what conditions they should labour, what they should think, what they should believe. Until comparatively recent times, except for occasional rebellions, the many suffered in silence and obeyed.

The notion of neo-colonialism is structured by power, but economic power rather than political power. And since power resides in the centre, it radiates by remote control to the periphery. For Cameroon and other African nations therefore, neo-colonialism can be said to have officially marked the transformation of their interdependence into dependency. That is, their economies and politics would henceforth be conditioned by a global economy dominated by others. Seen from this perspective, neo-colonialism can be seen as the root of political marginalization and economic exploitation in postcolonial Cameroon. But, neo-colonialism though carefully crafted and subtly implemented, could not have succeeded in Cameroon if not for the complicity and duplicity of high ranking Cameroonians.

Incidentally, Cameroonian intellectuals are among the first to react against the nefarious and execrable effects of neo-colonialism and to articulate the ways in which the monster can be tackled, or at least, contained. For example, Fonlon (2) proposes that, "Africa must unite, mobilize, to stem the tide of resurgent imperialism and to consolidate our political independence. This can only be done by loosening the foreign strangle-hold on our economies; we must develop and exploit our resources rationally."He goes further to suggest what Africans must do and have in order to liberate themselves.

> To achieve this we need two basic, fundamental, and absolutely indispensable means, namely, knowledge and capital. Of these, Knowledge is of greater importance in the order of things; for we all know that what has given the white man his overwhelming superiority in the world is science, and one of the greatest handicaps that barred the African's road to progress, was ignorance. Even in the political domain knowledge is of supreme importance; for, as Aristotle has stressed, good governance is not the work of chance but of science and purpose.

Fonlon is making two fundamental points in the above excerpts. Firstly, that Africans must take their destiny into their own hands. Secondly, that knowledge is power. That is, it is only through the possession of knowledge and skill that Africans can hope to achieve economic development. Chuba Okadigbo in (Ngeh, 247), on his part, agrees with Fonlon that Africans themselves must undertake the daunting task of salvaging their economy; but he goes further to caution them that the kind of freedom that they are agitating for is not given on a platter of gold. It has to be fought for.

> Freedom or liberty is hardly ever given; it is taken. The African must therefore fight for his freedom; take his liberty by himself for himself and for his kind. To do this, he must look before he leaps; think before he talks or writes. To free himself of alien ideologies designed by others for themselves and for the domination of others, the African has to design an ideological position, consistent with the past, conscious of his present and committed to his future.

Globalization

While African and Cameroonian scholars and thinkers are still floundering about what strategies to use to counter the negative effects of neo-colonialism, it gradually dawns on them that neo-colonialism is, actually, the tip of the ice-berg, a precursor to an even more sophisticated economic predator in the name of globalization. This is a concept of the 1990s and refers to the growing worldwide interdependence of peoples, cultures, and countries. It also connotes an artificial delineation of the world into two economic spheres: the economically viable North and the less developed countries of the South. Globalization is seen by many as the invisible and vulpine stage of imperialism. The Nigerian socio-linguist, Kayode-Iyasere in (Ngarka, 2008: 123) has described globalization "as the product of econometrical integration, where econometrical means economic imperialism predicated on the economic domination of the world by the industrialized nations". A good example of the psychology of globalization is found in Joseph Conrad's famous novel, *Nostromo* (1963:96-97) that book, the American Financier of the "House of Holroyd", in answer to a question from the protagonist about what the Third World is, says

> *It is the bottomless pit of 10 per cent loans and other fool investments. European capital has been flung into it with both hands for years. Not ours though. We in this country know just about enough to keep indoors when it rains. We can sit and watch. Of course, someday we shall step in. We are bound to. But there's no hurry. Time itself has got to wait on the greatest country in the whole of God's universe. We shall be giving the word for everything; industry, trade, law, journalism, art, politics and religion, from Cape Horn clear over to Smith's Sound and beyond, too, if anything worth taking hold of turns up at the North Pole. And then we shall have leisure in hand to take in hand the outlying islands and continents of the earth. We shall run the world's business whether the world likes it or not. The world can't help it – and neither can we, I guess.*

It is obvious from the tone of the American Financier in the above excerpt that the United States of America is not only exultant but also triumphant for being the world's only economic super-power. In the light of the above, there is the fear that globalization will eventually make differences to vanish thereby propelling the world towards a common objective and the predominance of a common culture.

Generally speaking, globalization has clear and widespread social and political implications and the arguments surrounding it are multi-faceted, complex, elusive and controversial. According to H.A. Asobie in (Ngarka, 123) globalization

> *is a contested concept, its meaning is in contention. Its character is a point in dispute. Its history is mired in controversy and although the ideological implications are relatively free of serious contestation, its implication for different geo-political zones of the international system constitute a moot point.*

The positive and negative consequences of globalization on the economically developed countries are too well known thanks to the advances in information and communication technologies. Therefore, it will not be necessary to repeat them here. Hence, I will limit myself to some of its positive and negative impact on the least developed countries with special emphasis on Cameroon.

Let me begin with the benefits. There is no doubt that globalization has increased the options of many Cameroonians and has multiplied their opportunities. For example, today, Cameroonians can travel around the world with ease. They can read current issues of the Financial Times, Washington Post, New York Times and Le Monde. They can send and receive money rapidly through Western Union and MoneyGram. They can send and receive express parcels through DHL and UPS. They can watch World News from a variety of Western and other channels - CNN, BBC, Euronews, France 24, Aljazeera, Press TV and Africa 24. Finally, they now live in a world of cyber space where they can communicate with people around the world through personal computer networks, cell phones, i-pods, e-mail, face book and the internet. But, as Campton in (Ngam, 270) has remarked, the social development of a people cannot be measured by technological advancements alone.

> *Increasingly, concern is being expressed that mankind's existence upon this globe will be contingent upon how quickly and how well we can discover and make use of ways and means for resolving the large-scale problems of poverty, ignorance, disease, and*

> civic inertia common to the majority of the world's population. At the root of this concern is a serious need to rethink our definition of development and the means by which we measure its attainment. Certainly, the measurement of development solely in terms of GNP is insufficient. We have come to realize that a much greater emphasis must be placed on the social and ecological conditions of development. We have learnt that social development does not automatically flow from economic improvement. We have found that the neglect of human problems in social-psychological terms and the systematic mutilation of the natural environment are loosening man from his age-old moorings. We are finally realizing that man cannot find his salvation in technology and concrete alone.

The implication of the above is that globalization does have its seamy side. The Cameroonian economy it will be recalled, is still predominantly agricultural. Yet Cameroonian cash crops: coffee, cocoa, tea, banana, rubber and cotton are firmly controlled by Western multinationals and mega corporations. They determine the prices on the world market and at the same time use the policy of protectionism to control access to the markets of the developed nations. By a perverted logic, the Cameroonian market is to remain wide open thus making the country a dumping ground for all types of Western products. Decisions about global finances are made in the economically developed countries while Cameroon though vitally affected by these unilateral decisions, stands by helplessly. Globalization has also eroded the Cameroonian political power base and Cameroonian politicians have been held hostage by the London and Paris clubs of (creditors) especially by the Bretton Woods Organizations. That is, the World Bank and the International Monetary Fund who impose the Structural Adjustment Programme, economic liberalism, free capital flow, free markets and deregulated banks among several other stiff economic measures and austerity programmes on Cameroon. They also coerce the government to privatize all key state owned enterprises whether they are viable or not. According to them, the primary goal of their privatization and commercialization programmes is to reduce the dominance of the public sector in the economy and allow the private sector to play its proper role as the leading engine of growth. But, instead of addressing what they referred to as the gross failure of these public enterprises to live up to expectations, privatization actually transferred ownership of these enterprises – Sonel (electricity), Camwater (water), Camrail (railway) etc to Western multinationals because Cameroonians are unable to raise the necessary capital to buy the enterprises. Thus, in Cameroon, globalization and privatization are seen as two sides of the same coin.

The economic life of Cameroon has also degenerated as a result of globalization. Hence, the country is experiencing the effects of protracted low GDP growth, high interest rates, intractable inflation, deteriorating exchange rates, and very little foreign direct investments. Finally, globalization is polluting the Cameroonian environment, undermining traditional mores, and sweeping away the notions of equality, egalitarianism and the laws of reciprocity which are the hall marks of development replacing them with the partnership of the horse and the rider.

To summarize, globalization has obviously brought with it the advancement of Western values and its idea of the organization of power, economy and society, among other things, into Cameroon. This spread of Western values, as I have demonstrated, has been driven by the exclusive interest of the West, often in contradistinction with the interest of Cameroonians. Thus, through the effective control of international institutions, organizations and structures, the economically developed countries have succeeded in imposing liberal democracy and economic reforms in countries like Cameroon which they consider strategic to their politico-economic interests. Of course, they show little or no regard to the negative consequences of their policies on Cameroonians. Seen in this light, globalization can be described as political and economic reforms engineered from "above" and "without". Hence, from the 1990s when the effects of globalization were first felt in Cameroon, the majority of Cameroonians have discovered much to their chagrin that instead of facilitating their efforts in the struggle for the good life, globalization has further compounded their problems. Hence, they find themselves powerless to fight this economic monster which is bent on subordinating their interests to those of Western capitalists.

It is therefore obvious from the above that globalization has both positive and negative aspects and that the latter far outweighs the former as far as Cameroon and the rest of the less developed countries of the world are concerned. Unfortunately, the process of globalization is much more complex than it appears at first sight. Furthermore, globalization turns out to be a complex phenomenon which has contradictions that can enlarge or degrade humanity. Nevertheless, it is an inexorable force that can neither be fought successfully nor stopped completely. This is where the dilemma of Cameroonians lie. They are expected to embrace the tenets of globalization and at the same time to remain local. That is, to maintain their identity in an international context. To complicate matters, they are expected to do that and, at the same time, cope with the heavy debt burden which is hanging on their necks like an albatross.

The point has already been made that globalization originated from the economically developed countries and is remotely controlled by them for their own interests. In other words, it is the economic recolonization of the developing world by the world's super powers. Therefore, it cannot, in its present configuration contribute to a meaningful development of the Third World. The fundamental question however remains, how can the Third World reach the much desired equilibrium in the New World Order created by globalization? The answer to this basic question is two-pronged. Firstly, the Third World cannot continue to blame others indefinitely for its woes. It must accept its own share of the blame and set about finding lasting solutions to its internecine economic problems. Secondly, since the world's super powers firmly control globalization, it is left to them to take the initiative if the Third World is to be truly integrated into the global mainstream. There are several things that the superordinate countries of the North can do to extricate the subordinate countries of the South from poverty, squalor, and disease. They can transform globalization into a veritable international engine that can ensure the material improvement of all the peoples of the world. That goal can be achieved by the implementation of a well-structured economic programme for the less developed countries of the world that hopefully will help to right the wrongs of many years of subjugation and servitude.

The point must however be made here that the developed countries have been making half-hearted attempts to address the problems of inequality through debt cancellation, the AGOA Initiative by the United States, the Heavily Indebted Poor Countries initiative and other cosmetic reparations. But the conditions which the Third World countries must fulfill in order to benefit from these measures are too stringent and therefore fall far too short of making the required impact. Accordingly, if the superordinate countries really want to bridge the widening gap separating them from the subordinate countries then they must resolutely address the sources of poverty and dependency that are leading to new forms of recolonization.

The Stake Holders
Having touched on some of the economic and political measures which the developed countries can take in favour of the less developed countries, I will now focus attention on what the developing countries can do for themselves using Cameroon as a case in point. To begin with, there is a consensus of opinion that for any meaningful change to occur, the impetus must come from within Cameroon and must be spearheaded by Cameroonians who know the problems of their people and who are committed to a set of social, political or ethical ideals. But, is there any goodwill and genuine commitment to collective betterment among Cameroonians? The answer appears to be in the negative. Cameroonians who are willing to be in the forefront of the progressive forces who are raising the level of political and cultural consciousness of

their compatriots are hard to find. Some of the politicians who have been entrusted with power are responsible for the imbroglio in which the country finds itself. The educated elite have either abjured responsibility or have aligned themselves with the politicians in power. The result is that they are condoning the excesses and abuses that they see. Indeed, they have turned out to be the embodiment and the very epitome of the petit bourgeoisie so vividly depicted by Karl Marx in (Gugelberger, 133):

> *The petty bourgeois is necessarily from his position a socialist on one side and an economist on the other; that is to say, he is dazed by the magnificence of the big bourgeoisie and has sympathy for the sufferings of the people. He is at once both bourgeois and man of the people. Deep down, in his heart he flatters himself that he is impartial and has found the right equilibrium, which claims to be something different from mediocrity... A petty bourgeois of this type glorifies contradiction because contradiction is the basis of his existence. He is himself nothing but social contradiction in action.*

The economists who, because of their professional training, are expected to contribute to a better understanding of the country's endemic developmental problems have been mesmerized by the complexities of the global economy and have been diverted to withdrawing into themselves. In that respect, they are no different from the educated petit bourgeois class. That is understandable since they are all products of the imperialist educational system. Lenin in (Gugelberger, 133) attempts to unmask the class roots of bourgeois scholarship:

> *Not a single one of these bourgeois professors, who are capable of making very valuable contributions in the special fields of chemistry, history or physics can be trusted one iota when it comes to philosophy. Why? For the same reason that not a single professor of political economy, who may be capable of very valuable contributions in the field of factual and specialized investigations, can be trusted one iota when it comes to the general theory of political economy. For in modern society the latter is as much a*

> *partisan science as is epistemology. Taken as a whole, the professors of economics are nothing but learned salesmen of the capitalist class, while the professors of philosophy are learned salesmen of the theologians.*

It is therefore not surprising that the masses are suspicious and apprehensive of the educated class who constitute the petit bourgeoisie especially for its failure to deliver the promise of a commitment to emancipate the people from exploitation and oppression. As Michael Vaughan remarks in (Gugelberger, 218),

> *The petty bourgeoisie is seen as having revoked its obligation to devote itself to the improvement of the poor and oppressed majority... - it has betrayed this obligation by preoccupying itself with consumerism, display and degenerate appetites. This class is profoundly untrustworthy because, though it employs when the occasion suits it a language of popular rhetoric, its real impetus is acquisitive and rapacious: 'you know, people don't trust the educated because they hunt with the wolves and graze with the sheep mostly.'*

The political opposition parties themselves seem to do very little to sustain the momentum and enthusiasm for positive change that has been engendered by the rebirth of multi-party politics in the country. Francis B. Nyamnjoh (1999:114) suggests that,

> *It seems as though the general concern of the opposition parties is to substitute the ruling bellies, and not the wellbeing of everyone. Again, the quarrel of the opposition is more with the eaters than with the eating, as those of them who have managed to get themselves involved in government have quickly fallen prey to the comforts of chaos. Denunciations of malpractice in high office, by the opposition, appear more and more as political gimmicks, as even the most radical of them have not sought to go beyond what Monga has termed 'slogans in line with populist illusions'. The opposition has failed to inspire or sustain popular hope either in the way opposition leaders managed their intra- and inter-party differences on the one hand, and their Councils on the*

> *other, or in the way they have conducted themselves in parliament.*

The ordinary Cameroonians who are the direct victims of exploitation and marginalization cannot take their destiny into their own hands because of apathy and cynicism. In the final analysis only the literary artists of the oral and written traditions remain perhaps because they are finding it difficult to escape from the responsibility of serving their people; or perhaps because they are aware that literature, whether oral or written must find a place in the revolution which must sweep their country. That may explain why they are re-examining their themes, their outlook on society, their language, and their manner of presentation.

Let me begin with the modern Cameroonian writers. Bernard Nanga, Mongo Beti, Pabe Mongo, Charly-Gabriel Mbock, David Ndache Tagne, Bole Butake, Ghalia Gwangwa'a, Bate Besong, Gilbert Doho, Nol Alembong, Joseph Kengni, Emmanuel Fru Doh, John N. Nkengasong, Victor Epie Ngome, Alobwed'Epie, Ngong Kum Ngong, and Oscar Labang to name just these. They are all astute social critics and articulate political commentators who believe in the direct relationship between literature and social institutions. They are convinced that the principal function of literature especially in the developing world is to criticize these social institutions in order to bring about acceptable changes in society. For example, addressing his audience on his website, http:// gahliagwangwaa.com, the Anglophone Cameroonian poet, Gahlia Gwangwa'a declares:

> *I will continue to talk and write about it until something is done. I write for those who have eyes and cannot see. For those who have voices but cannot speak out. I will, with my pen, defend them courageously to the end. Through my pen, the plight of Cameroonians will be brought to light for the world to see.*

Seen from this perspective, they can be said to be writing what Mao Tse-Tung (in Gugelberger, 59) has described as revolutionary literature.

> *Revolutionary literature and art should create a variety of characters out of real life and help the masses to propel history forward. For example, there is suffering from hunger, cold and oppression on the one hand, and exploitation and oppression of man by man on the other. These facts exist everywhere and people look upon them as common place. Writers and artists concentrate such everyday phenomena, typify the contradictions and struggles within them and produce works which awaken the masses, fire them with enthusiasm and impel them to unite and struggle to transform their environment.*

While these writers can be considered as being fully committed to the cause of the ordinary people, their actions are ultimately futile and symbolic. Firstly, because they write in European languages thereby ignoring the problem of mass illiteracy in Cameroon. In other words, they write an elitist literature mainly for a coterie of literates in the society. Secondly, because their autonomy has been eroded in a capitalist society. That is, their artistic freedom and their products have been subjected to the whims and caprices of the market.

Finally, the unjust political system which they criticize has an effective way of censoring them. That explains, in part, why most of the writers mentioned above either have fled into physical exile in Europe or the United States of America, or have chosen to remain in Cameroon and assume a position of mental alienation.

About Popular/Protest Musicians

The profiles of the popular/protest musicians selected for study in this book are clearly related to a conception of what life in Cameroon is like for the dispossessed and marginalized population. The musicians encapsulate the basic conditions of the majority of Cameroonians. They do not belong to the class of small, well-educated elite which is widely separated from the rest of the people in terms of its educational provision. In fact, none of them holds a university degree, and none of them had a great start in life. They are all self-taught. They have virtually no sponsors and receive little or no encouragement from the ruling elite. In fact, by criticizing the corrupt political system for betraying the people, they unwittingly put themselves on the firing line. All of them have become centres of controversy and victims of constant harassment.

Most of them were obliged to begin their musical careers in bars, cabarets, and nightclubs. Since they could not possibly live on the proceeds of their music, most of them had to explore their talents in various ways. For example, Martin Tohmutan Tubuo, alias Prince Yerima Afo Akom has taken to tailoring as an alternative profession. Longkana Agno Simon, alias Longue Longue is a carpenter when he is not engaged in music. And Lambo Pierre Roger Sandjo, popularly known as Lapiro de Mbanga owns a nightclub. Thus, they are all self-made and self-supporting.

In the absence of legitimate conditions of political activity in the country, the functions of protest music naturally overlapped with politics. That explains why the protest songs are directed more towards castigating the powerful forces and raising the consciousness of the people than towards entertainment. That is, the songs have become politically prescriptive.

The political history of Cameroon from the colonial period to contemporary times has been intentionally biased in favour of a few spineless individuals who served as lackeys of the colonial administration. These minions and servile conformists have been deliberately glorified and projected into prominence by their colonial masters while many heroes and martyrs who have sacrificed their lives for their fatherland and by whose sacrifice wars were fought and independence won, have been consciously relegated into oblivion. It is therefore in an attempt to rewrite the history of Africa in general and Cameroon in particular, and to rehabilitate these unsung heroes and patriots that the protest musicians have taken the bold step to include in their songs such ultranationalists as Martin Paul Samba, Douala Manga Bell, Ruben Um Nyobe, Felix Moumie and Ernest Ouandie from Cameroon. They include: Patrice Lumumba from the Democratic Republic of Congo; Thomas Sankara from Burkina Faso; Kwame Nkrumah from Ghana;

and Nelson Mandela and Steve Biko from South Africa. The modus vivendi of the protest musicians is momentous in the sense that it provides bench marks for proper conduct, sacrifice, and leadership in Cameroon and Africa. Besides, a proper recognition of these torch bearers provides practical lessons for national consciousness, unity, integration and development. Finally, it also inspires responsible leadership and patriotism among the youths who, according to the musicians should make a difference by cleansing Cameroon and Africa of corrupt and unpatriotic individuals who are a permanent threat to the precarious peace in the continent.

Most of the protest musicians invariably allude to the city of Bamenda in their songs. That is understandable. Bamenda, the capital of the North West Region is noted for its intransigence and volatility. The people themselves are politically hypersensitive, tempestuous, and aggressive. Bamenda is also the birthplace of such archetects of the Reunification of Cameroon as John Ngu Foncha and Solomon Tandeng Muna. Futhermore, both the ruling CPDM party and the frontline opposition party, the SDF were launched in Bamenda. All these factors contribute in making Bamenda the political melting pot of Cameroon.

The philosophy of the protest musicians can be said to be Marxist in orientation because of the artists' commitment to the social cause, and because the songs are used to criticize injustices in society in the hope of eventually bringing about desirable social, economic, and political change in the country. The musicians are neither hoarders nor accumulators. If anything, they are givers and sharers. In that respect, they exemplify the virtues of communalism.

One aspect that distinguishes the selected protest musicians is their linguistic virtuosity. Prince Yerima Afo Akom sings in English, French, Pidgin English, Hausa, and Kom his home language. Longue Longue combines French, Pidgin English, Douala, and his own neologisms. And Lapiro sings in French, Pidgin English, and Camfranglais. Hence, all the musicians are veritable polyglots. This language mixing is a conscious act by the musicians intended to reach a wider audience made up essentially of the common people, to avoid the risk of being arrested by trigger-happy law enforcement officers, and to underscore the plurilugal nature of the country. Lapiro, the foremost Cameroonian protest musician is also the most successful linguistic innovator. He created the now famous urban lingo known as Lapiroism. According to Peter Vakunta (2010:3),

> *Lapiroism became popular in Cameroon between 1990 and 1992, an era associated with the emergence of opposition political parties. An impressionistic inspection of fluent speakers of Lapiroisms reveals that they are pedlars, taximen, bendskinneurs, wheelcart pushers, hawkers, prostitutes, vagabonds, thieves, prisoners, gamblers, conmen, musicians and comedians. The lexical and, relexification, and dysphemistic extensions characteristic of Lapiroisms reflect the provocative attitude of its speakers and their jocular disrespect of linguistic norms and purity clearly revealing its function as an anti-language.*

Lapiro himself describes his music differentiated by this composite language as an armament against oppression: "Music is a sort of weapon; sometimes instead of using guns, you use music, you use the voice, you use the sound and people who are against freedom will be shot down by your lyrics, by your sound, by your musical attitude"(Vakunta,6). Vakunta sums up his appreciation of Lapiro thus:

> *Lapiro de Mbanga is an anti-establishment songwriter. He is both an entertainer and social critic. His danceable lyrics are both hosannas of hope and lamentations of the socially ostracized. He takes jibes at Cameroon's morally bankrupt leaders exemplified by dereliction of duty. His lyrics have an evocative appeal on an array of music connoisseurs on both sides of the Mungo River. Lapiro's success in creating a novel lingo bears testimony to the extraordinary intellect of this self-taught musician. His songs have produced a tonic effect on a new generation of young Cameroonian musicians. Committed musicians like Longue Longue are producing musical compositions that call into question, impunity, administrative*

> *arrogance, bad governance, corruption, influence pedling, and other social ills that impede social progress and economic development in Cameroon. Lapiroism is a lethal tool wielded with dexterity by this polyglot singer in his head-on vendetta against the nation's grave-diggers.*

This apposite description of Lapiro can also to a very large extent apply to all the protest musicians discussed in this book. All of them see their music as a strong weapon against inept and opportunistic leadership. All of them use their music to exhort members of the petit bourgeoisie to remember the cause of 'the People'. All of them also use their music to encourage the masses to stand up for their rights.

The protest musicians under consideration in this book, as I have established above, are actually the parallels of the modern writers mentioned earlier. I have also substantiated the fact that they are intrepid socio-political commentators with a clear conception of their society and what that society expects of them. That explains why they produce songs that are essentially realistic and even didactic. But, I also made the point that, unlike the modern Cameroonian writers who write for a relatively small educated audience, the oral artists produce for a mass audience which is virtually ready-made. The reasons for this situation are not hard to find. Unlike the modern writers who are separated from the ordinary people by virtue of their education and social status, the oral artists are an integral part of the masses. That is, they live and move and have their being in society. They speak the language that the people understand, use the expression that the people appreciate, and create their works for the good of their society. In other words, they produce what is usually considered as popular or protest music. George Thomson (65) is referring to this role of the oral artist when he says that , "the poet speaks not for himself but for his fellow men. His cry is their cry, which only he can utter. That is what gives it its depth. But if he is to speak for them, he must suffer with them, rejoice with them, work with them, fight with them." Finally, they are able, for the most part, to escape official censorship and police harassment because their linguistic hodge-podge may pose comprehension difficulties to the uninitiated. For example, popular or protest songs are aired over national radio and television and are enjoyed by everybody regardless of social status. The fact however remains that whether the words are understood or not, they are integral to the language of the people. As McDaniels in (Ngam, 264) reminds us using the example of the folktale,

> *Folktales permit people to express emotions in a socially approved manner that would be inappropriate in any other form. The acceptance of popular lingo and non-standard expressions is commonplace and actually enriches folktales. People can engage in projective fantasy by creating tales that contain realistic themes, using symbolism and metaphoric projections on both the unconscious and the conscious cultures.*

So far, I have attempted an overview of the origin and evolution of Power and Marginality in the Third World in general and in Cameroon in particular. I have also examined the roles of the different stakeholders in the game of Power, and outlined what each of them can do to bridge the gap between those who hold power and those who are victims of the rapacious use of power. Finally, I have made the point that the oral artists are best placed to use their artistic skills to help in the delicate and daunting task of off-setting the balance of power in favour of the marginalized majority. I intend to demonstrate this fact in the chapters that follow using selected oral tales, proverbs, and popular or protest songs.

Theoretical Consideration

I intend in this book to correlate the orature under study to its social background in order to determine how the intentions and attitudes of the oral artists issue out of the wider social contexts of their works. In doing so, I will treat the orature as literature and I will also bear in mind Neil Skinner's suggestion in (Tala, 1999: 6) that:

> *In judging any literature it is of primary importance to determine what standards of criticism should be used in the discussions. To do this we must first ask what we*

are trying to do with the literature. And the answer surely is that we are trying to understand the literature and develop techniques by which to communicate this understanding to others.

My concern here is however not limited to the standards of criticism to be used in evaluating the orature under discussion. Rather, it is more with what literary theory I should use since both "literature" and "theory" are concepts that are foreign to Africa. Furthermore, how can these Western concepts be domesticated so that they can be applied to the interpretation of African orature? Let me begin with the concept of "literature". Rene Wellek in (Opata, 2000: 220), identifies four fields of meaning in which the term "literature" is used. According to him,

> *There is literature without distinction of subject matter but with the implication of quality, aesthetic, intellectual, moral, or political. Below it, we may say, are all writings, historical, political, philosophical, critical, and didactic, that do not reach the level of inclusion in a national literature. I am afraid that the writings of most scholars and critics belong to this second category. Then there is the other meaning of literature as imaginative literature, which I will set off by the concept of "fictionality" and confess the failure of making the distinction one of a special literary language. This descriptive meaning includes bad fiction, or whatever we call sub-literature, which is well worth study as a social document for the history of taste. It fulfils a social function that we may deplore as escapism or welcome as satisfying human aesthetic urges. And finally, there is the realm of imaginative literature in which the aesthetic function dominates.*

From Wellek's perspective then, literature is something that is either oral or written. It is everything that is written. It is imaginative, fictional, and employs a special literary language. Finally, it is created to serve an aesthetic function. Although Wellek is speaking from the point of view of Western literary tradition, what he says has some bearings on African orature. Nevertheless, he has ignored the functional and ideological nature of literature which are crucial to an understanding of

African orature. Literary theory, on the other hand, is a set of principles used in interpreting and evaluating a literary work. Virtually all the literary theories that are extant today, have been specifically designed for the evaluation of contemporary Western literature with emphasis on aesthetic quality. In other words, an African literary theory is yet to come into being. Nevertheless, the Western theories can, with some modifications, be applied to the study of modern African literature. The question then is, what theory should be used in the study of African orature considering the fact that it is functional and politically prescriptive, and that the context of its production and consumption is different from the context of production and consumption of modern African literature? One scholar has attempted an answer:

> *Oral literature as the reflection of human intellects takes place in complex social situations which need to be discerned. Its popular appeal can be maintained so long as it meets people's expectations. The analysis of oral narrative should not be deviated from the way the members of a community perceive it. The formation of its representative meanings, their interpretations, and the manipulation of genres depend on social realities. This means the acceptability of the verbal art and their meanings ensure their effective functions in the society, whereas the deviation from them threatens their existence in the modern world. "A literary work is not an object that stands by itself and that offers the same view to each reader in each period. It is not a monument that monologically reveals its timeless essence. It is much more like an orchestration that strikes ever new resonances among its readers and that brings it to a contemporary existence". The skilful manipulation of forms in social interaction, the capability of performing them in accordance with the existing social climate and the meticulous scrutiny of the interplay between people's needs and folklore practices are the basis for the dynamic functions of the verbal genres. The expectations the society has towards the narrator (performer), the appropriateness of the subject in the changing social, historical and political circumstances*

> *are points of primary concern in the analysis of folklore in modern context. In other words, the social status of the community members, their knowledge, eloquence and personal quality secure the pertinence of folklore language to the situation. (www.sdu.dk/-/media)*

Two points stand out clearly from this rather lengthy quotation. The first is that orature is functional and is socially conditioned. That is, it mirrors cultural values and expresses socially accepted ideas. It heightens and intensifies the most important concerns of the people, and it is a direct commentary on how things are in the society or how they ought to be.

The second is that performance is an important concept in the formulation, interpretation and evaluation of orature. It gives the oral literary artist the opportunity to exercise his skill in deploying verbal and non-verbal elements appropriate to his chosen medium and vision. It also provides the audience the basis on which to appreciate the creativity and originality of the oral literary artist.

Unfortunately, several Western literary critics and Western trained African literary critics are not comfortable with the emphasis on the functionality of African orature for the simple reason that it entails the bringing in of extra-textual material in the analysis of the orature. In the opinion of these well-meaning but misdirected literary critics, polemicism compromises aesthetic quality, and art that is functional is bad art. That is rather unfortunate because as Edward Said in (Gagiano, 15) has explained,

> *Criticism cannot assume that its province is merely the text, not even the great literary text. It must see itself, with other discourse, inhabiting a much more contested cultural space, in which what has counted in the continuity and transmission of knowledge has been the signifier, as an event that has left lasting traces upon the human subject. Once we take that view, then literature as an isolated paddock in the broad cultural field disappears, and with it too the harmless rhetoric of self-delighting humanism. Instead, we will be able, I think, to read and write with a sense of the greater stake in historical and political effectiveness that literary as well as other texts have had.*

From the standpoint of the oral literary artists, good art is art which serves the purposes of the people; and a good literary artist is one who experiments with form until he is able to achieve a unity of form and content in his oral piece. The implication here is that the literary concerns - the thematic priorities and their attendant idioms - of the oral literary artists and their public are vastly different from those of Western writers and their audience. Furthermore, there is no valid evidence to show that aesthetic quality is antithetical to social determinism.

Orature, as I have already remarked, has both form and content. But critical emphasis has been placed more on form than on content. My argument here is that in order to understand and evaluate a piece of orature adequately, the critic needs to go beyond the form. He must consider the socio-cultural and political contexts in which the piece of orature is created, its structure, audience participation, thematic content, the literary and dramatic devices employed by the oral literary artist among other things. Since none of the existing Western literary theories can treat the above elements holistically and adequately, and in the absence of a clearly formulated African literary theory, I am left with very little choice but to adopt the New Historicist and the Postcolonial theory. The use of the eclectic approach is in keeping with Ambanasom 's(16) view expressed below:

> *No single approach is valid for all works. No matter its claims and supposed validity one should not carry a single approach blindly to a work of art; it is rather the work that calls forth the type of approach suitable for its apprehension. An approach that is only remotely relevant to a work of art may mislead its conceiver to condemn the creative writer for the wrong crime; it may force the critic to judge and crucify the artist for what he never set out to do in the first place.*

The two literary theories: New Historicism and Post-colonial theory suggest themselves by virtue of the title of this book. New Historicists, for example, hold that intrinsic and extrinsic factors are essential for an interpretation of a work of art. That is, art is not created in a vacuum. Put differently, it is a representation of the society from which it emanates. This view is shared by Chinweizu et al (1983:253), especially when they assert that:

> *Art's relations to society are very important, and that the investigation of these relationships may organize and deepen one's aesthetic response to the work of art. Art is not created in a vacuum; it is the work not simply of a person, but of an author fixed in time and space, answering to a community of which he is an important and articulate part.*

Since New Historicism cannot possibly cover all the expectations of this book, I am complementing it with Postcolonial theory. As a literary theory, Post colonialism deals with art and literature produced in countries that were once colonized by European powers; in the case of Cameroon, - Britain, France, and Germany. From the critical perspective, the theory sets out not only to destabilize Western ways of thinking and to create space for the marginalized groups to challenge inherent assumptions, but also to produce alternatives to the dominant discourse. The two theories are therefore relevant to the purposes of this book because the issues which the protest musicians grapple with are linked both to the colonial past and the new challenges facing Cameroon.

In order to achieve the objectives of this study therefore, I have divided this book into five chapters, an Introduction and a Conclusion. The introduction lays the foundation on which the general discussion is based. It comprises the aims of the study, the definition of key terms and the structure of the book.

Chapter one is titled "Literature and Society". It examines the intricate relationship existing between orature and society in contemporary Cameroon with emphasis on the dynamics of power relations within Cameroon's rather complex political life. It also examines the contestative nature of orature in order to emphasize its suitability for criticizing the status quo and for indicating the way forward for the country.

Chapter two, titled "Orature and Ethological Education", is concerned with the educational functions of orature. It criticizes the maleficent colonial system of education which Cameroon inherited at independence and which is yet to be adapted to the changing realities of the country. It posits that the deliberate neglect of orature in the curriculum, has led to the rapid decline in the ethological aspects of the education offered in Cameroon since independence and that, in turn, has led to the imbroglio in which Cameroon finds itself today. It argues that since adults, who are supposed to teach by precepts have abdicated their responsibility to their country, it is left to the younger generation to take over. Hence, the need for them to be taught their orature because it emphasizes the correct and acceptable moral conduct of the society.

Chapter three of this book is titled "Popular Songs and Perceptions of Nationhood". It examines orature set in the present and dealing with contemporary Cameroonian political realities. But it does this from the perspective of the ordinary people. It demonstrates that the relations between the "majority" and the "minority" groups have existed in the political life of all countries and, therefore, the ascendancy claims in intergroup relations can be considered as normal. However, it becomes a tragedy when the successive postcolonial governments in Cameroon insist on pursuing a policy of divide and rule by favoring the claims and interests of the minority power holders over the majority of the population whom they govern. It makes the point that the appropriate and realistic form of governance which a pluralistic country like Cameroon needs is one that can ensure a level playing ground for its constituent ethnic tribes. Finally, it advocates the attendance to the voices of the underrepresented segments of the society and the use of power with responsibility.

Chapter four is titled "The Political Economy of Dependency" and focuses on the economic imbalance in the country caused by pervasive corruption and the rapacious use of power; and the disadvantaged position which Cameroon occupies as a result of globalization. It examines why, in spite of the efforts and financial resources invested in development projects in Cameroon, the results have been below expectations. It posits that one important reason is that development projects are not premised on cultural conditions. It is from that standpoint that it suggests that if the situation is to improve, both Cameroonian development planners and their foreign partners must recognize the role of indigenous knowledge in development programmes. They must also be prepared to adopt the participatory approach to development. As concerns the present economic imbalance in the country, it insists that in order to offset the gross trade imbalance, the initiative must be taken by Cameroonians themselves. But, in the long run, the real efforts at bridging the economic gap separating the developed countries and Cameroon must be made by the developed countries for the simple reason that they pull the economic strings in the world.

Chapter five "The Way Forward" discusses some of the solutions which the protest musicians have advanced for the problems bedevilling Cameroon and the strategies which they propose for salvaging the country. It singles out corruption for special treatment and concludes that the scourge may be contained but can hardly be eliminated entirely.

The Conclusion summarizes the main arguments, and states my findings and recommendations.

CHAPTER ONE
LITERATURE AND SOCIETY

> *Art and society are thus necessarily connected: no art has been unaffected by social influences and no art has failed to influence society. No society has renounced its right to possess its own art and its consequent right to influence art. Art is almost as old as man himself: that is, almost as old as society. (Adolfo Sanchez Vazquez, 1973:113)*

Scholars have long since recognized the relationship between literature and society, but they have not fully appreciated how the Cameroonian society influences its orature and is in turn influenced by that orature. One scholar who has attempted an appreciation of the symbiotic relationship between literature and society is Vazquez (116). According to him, "In a world in which everything is quantified and abstracted, art: the highest form of expression of everything concrete and quantitative in human life: enters into a contradiction with the alienated world, becoming an incorruptible stronghold of humanity. Art and society thus become radically opposed. Art representing denied humanity, opposes an inhuman society". The implication here is that orature provides a true mirror of society because its themes, subject matter and formal development are determined by the cultural tradition and environment. These facts might have led Vazquez (112) to conclude that:

> *Each society gets the art it deserves, both because of the art it favors or tolerates, and because artists as members of society, create in accordance with the particular type of relations they have with that society. This means that art and society, far from finding themselves in a relation of mutual externality or indifference, either seek each other out or avoid one another, meet or separate, but can never completely turn backs on each other.*

This direct relationship between orature and society is seen in the functions which orature performs in society. As Vidjennagni Zounmenou in (Ngam, 2) submits, "whatever their weaknesses are, it appears that oral traditions, nonetheless, shape and promote moral order and ethical values, provide human understanding, facilitate elimination of anti-social behavior and help in the construction of social identity". The point being made here is that orature, as the living literature of the majority of Cameroonians ultimately derives its raw material from the realities of the society and hence reflects the values and world view of the people. It is also often used as a vehicle for transmitting and preserving their history, values and collective knowledge and experience. But, as Ngugi wa Thiong'o argues in *Writers in Politics* (1997:6),

> *Literature is more than just a mechanistic reflection of social reality. As part of man's artistic activities, it is in itself part of man's self-realization as a result of his wrestling with nature... It is a symbol of man's activity, of man's historical process of being and becoming... It does shape our attitudes of life to the daily struggles with nature, the daily struggles with the community, and daily struggles with individual souls and selves.*

The point Ngugi is making is that "all art aims to evoke; to awaken in the observer, the listener or reader emotions and impulses to action or opposition" (6). Thus, it can be said that there exists a direct relationship between orature and social institutions and, as I shall demonstrate in subsequent chapters, one of the main functions of orature, as far as the theme of this book is concerned, is social criticism for the improvement of the society.

Pre-capitalist Cameroon society, it will be recalled, is small scale, relatively self-sufficient, non-literate, rural and agricultural. Its social relationships are enduring because social change is evolutionary rather than revolutionary. The society itself subsists on the social philosophy of the greatest good of the greatest number. In other words, collective responsibility is the very essence of traditional authority. Hence, man in that society is less an autonomous individual than in the Western sense. This is because the society, according to Olatunde Odetola (in Ngam,208), puts "more emphasis on the group rather than on the individual, more on solidarity than on the activity and needs of the individual, more on the communion of persons than on their autonomy".

Traditional authority in Cameroon is understandably variegated and it is not at all surprising that scholars are sometimes bewildered by the range and variety of the political systems. However, what is of interest here is not the sequence of the political systems but the perceptions of power, especially the measures taken by the people to check leadership improprieties. The Nso society of the Grassfields region of Cameroon for example, is communal and cohesive in nature. It is well integrated and is governed by its well-tried mores, laws, sanctions and taboos. The Nso people are well grounded in the principles of political conduct. That is why they acknowledge the fact that in all human society, there is bound to be conflict which can eventually generate a series of socio-political problems. But, they also believe that irrespective of what the problem is, its resolution must take into account the welfare of the clan. Hence the proverb, "no man however great can be greater than his people". A person's place in society, his rights, duties, capabilities and privileges are clearly defined. That is why the people expect every Nso person to know and acknowledge when he is wrong. This idea is summed up in the saying "admitting one's errors is not a mark of cowardice but wisdom".

As in traditional cultures throughout the Grassfields region of Cameroon, the Fonship of Nso is a monolithic and sacred institution which is incarnated in the person of the Crown Prince. It is also hereditary. But the institution of the Fon is not the person per se. Rather, it is the traditional paraphernalia associated with the royal office like the ancestral stool "kava", the royal cup, and other traditional regalia which are regarded as the living symbols of traditional authority. Aletum Tabuwe and Fisiy Fonyuy (1989: 34) had this to say about the myth surrounding traditional authority in Nso:

> *In the palace in Nso, all initiated persons paid tribute and respected all rules of traditional etiquette to an empty royal stool even though the Fon was not seated on it. In fact, he was absent from the palace at that moment. This clear manifestation of respect results from*

> *the fact that the people consider the stool as the living symbol of traditional authority.*

The Fon is considered by his people both as the acknowledged repository of traditional authority and as the temporal representative of the supernatural order. As a result, his body is sacrosanct. Thus, the Fon of Nso occupies a composite office comprising political, spiritual, administrative and legislative functions. In spite of this concentration of powers in the person of the Fon however, his subjects still see him more as a father and a leader than as a ruler. Consequently, they have certain expectations of him. For example, their perception of power is that it should go hand in hand with responsible leadership. As a result, they expect their Fon to show great concern for their welfare. They also expect him to organize his administration in such a way that it responds positively to their collective aspirations. Hence the proverb, "anyone who says that he is leading and there is nobody following him, is only taking a walk." The demand by the people of Nso for good governance, is in accord with the argument advanced by Judith van Allen in (Furniss, 54) that

> *The handling of political matters requires a system in which public policy is made publicly and the relevant knowledge shared widely; in another sense, it entails the settling of questions that concern the welfare of the community in a public way (and therefore) necessitates the sharing of political knowledge – the knowledge needed for participation in political discussion and decisions.*

Thus, in Nso, as in other Grassfields chiefdoms, the actions of the Fon are discussed in the open in order to ensure that they meet the expectations of the people as far as peace, stability, accountability and development are concerned. The following story is about a traditional ruler who is living according to the dictates of tradition and who is concerned about the well-being of his people.

Achuo the Wise Chief

Achuo was always surrounded by his traditional councilors and elders who advised him on important issues concerning the welfare of the village. He listened to them and gradually became wise and popular. For quite some time, all the neighbouring villages were embroiled in inter-tribal wars over land. Chief Achuo was the only one who refused to engage in the senseless wars because he believed in the force of argument rather than in the argument of force. Even when he was provoked by the other chiefs or was branded as weak, he kept his calm. He even tried to broker peace between some of the belligerent chiefdoms but was ignored.

While the other chiefs were concentrating on war and its consequences, Chief Achuo spent his time developing his village. His people grew more food and had sufficient time for leisure. With time, the warring villages were struck by famine. They started searching for food desperately. As the famine began to take its toll, the villages swallowed their pride and sent their women to beg for food from Chief Achuo's village. The women were impressed by what they saw. The children, the crops, and the animals were healthy. The village was developed, and the people were visibly happy and satisfied. They were even more surprised by the hospitality and generosity of their hosts. There and then, they decided to go back and educate their chiefs about the foolishness of war and the advantages of peaceful co-existence. Fortunately, the chiefs listened to them and adopted peaceful negotiations in place of open confrontation as the best means of resolving their differences. That is how Chief Achuo became famous among his peers as a crusader of peace and development (Adapted from Ngam, 403-405).

The story of Chief Achuo is often told to buttress the fact that in traditional Grassfields society, the people have a say in the affairs of the village and how their lives are to be governed. They hold morality in high esteem. Hence, they make sure that whatever they do is motivated by what is in the interest of the village. The traditional mores ensure mutual co-existence for all. The system of government is naturally interwoven with these mores. Thus, the action of a chief is guided by a community oriented thinking. A good chief is one who listens to his people, who allows the freedom of expression, and who knows that his power is limited by the sovereign will of his people. That explains why the Fon is conscious of his responsibilities. He knows that he has to rely on his people and their social institutions for effective administration. As a result, he listens to their advice and complaints. As Kaberry in (Aletum, 36) has observed,

> *The Fon himself often says: "what is a Fon without people? I am in the hands of my people" and the Nso has two sayings which epitomize their conception of chieftainship: "The Fon has everything; the Fon is a poor man", and "the Fon rules the people, but the people hold the Fon".*

The Fon also knows that the traditional system has its checks and balances and so is careful to remain within the bounds of his authority. Commenting on the Nso polity in the North West Region of present day Cameroon, P.M. Kaberry in (Aletum, 35) has this to say:

> *The chieftainship is not a despotism. Though the Fon is paramount and has the right to initiate and to make the final decision in all matters affecting the country, he is also responsible for and accountable to his people. He is a source of welfare and wellbeing, and when he acts in a way that threatens the welfare of the country, he may be called to account as a person, for his authority is not of an impersonal kind as is that of Ngweron.*

Several scholars have written about the politicization of African orature. At the forefront of these scholars is Ruth Finnegan (1970:82) who posits that "the patronage of poets in centralized political systems in the past led to the creation of a poetry of political significance as a means of political propaganda, pressure or communication; such poetry includes songs of insult, challenge or satirical comment used as politically effective weapons". Thus, when a traditional authority refuses to respect the publicly accepted principles of political conduct, the people resort to the use of political poetry to censure such an errant ruler. Kofi Agovi in (Furniss, 58-59) paints a good picture of how the people of Nzema in Ghana use the Avudwene to criticize poor governance. In the following song, a chief who has been too spineless to resist the corrupting influence of both privilege and power, is subjected to scathing criticism by the Avudwene performers acting as voice of the voiceless majority.

> *It has been said that people show*
> *Courtesy to chiefs out of respect;*
> *We agreed to respect your office*
> *in anticipation of exemplary leadership.*
> *In this alone, we knew what we were doing.*
> *You have done well,*
> *Koasi Amakyi the imbecile,*
> *You have done well in this state.*
> *Since you have put on*
> *A fool's carrying-pad, you will*
> *Always carry a fool's burden!*
> *May the public listen to what we say;*
> *Our ancestors invoked this proverb*
> *and left it to posterity. They said:*
> *"If you ensnare gossip, you trap litigation.'*
> *The backwardness of Nzema*
> *Is all your fault, Koasi Amakyi.*
> *It was in earnest when it was said*
> *that truth is an eternal tree.*
> *Since you abhor the truth,*
> *we are suffering for your misdeeds...*
> *Because you only pursue the purse,*
> *You have created your own chiefs...*
> *Truly, Koasi Amakyi,*
> *You have done well in the state;*
> *May you uphold the truth this year*
> *so that we have peace again.*

The performers of the above song express the anger of the people against their chief who, because of greed and graft, is out of touch with his people's aspirations. The fact that they refer to their chief using his name, "Koasi Amakyi" is a deliberate act of disrespect bordering on insult. It is also an indication to the chief that no matter how much power he may wield, he is not above being called to order by his people. It is worth noting that the performers do not express their anger directly. Rather, they use satire to castigate the deviant chief.

This is expressed in the epithet "imbecile" and also in the following lines:
> You have done well,
> Koasi Amakyi the imbecile,
> You have done well in this state.
> Since you have put on a fool's carrying-pad, you will
> Always carry a fool's burden.

The performers go on to warn the chief of the dire consequences that await him for forfeiting the loyalty and respect of his people. They also use the proverb "if you ensnare gossip, you trap litigation" to remind him that in life, one always reaps what one sows. In spite of the vehement attack on the chief however, neither the performers nor the general public whom they represent want to dethrone him. Instead, they attempt, through the spirited criticism of his ineffective leadership, to rehabilitate him. That is why they advise him to "uphold the truth this year so that we can have peace again".

The main political issues in the traditional artistic forms that I have discussed so far, have been aptly summarized in the following excerpt by Agovi in (Furniss, 60):
> *The main issues are issues of governance. There are discourses on leadership, on sovereignty and power, and on the place of consent in political relations. There are issues of freedom of expression, openness, accountability and probity... Such serious concerns are expressed on behalf of society in the shared belief that public interest, and not the narrow interests of some constituted political authority, provides the main impetus for the performance always.*

Nso is a centralized state. But, what applies to it can, with slight modifications also apply to stateless, middle-sized and other forms of traditional polity all over Africa. Thus, whatever the political system, there are always inherent control mechanisms to bring deviants to order.

In traditional Cameroonian society then, environment is character. That is, the individual is what the society makes of him. But, the society itself is basically acquisitive and, to some extent, competitive. Therefore, it has to rely very much on its system of social controls to ensure internal order and cohesion.

One of the tried and tested instruments of social control is, its orature.

But, the misuse of power in traditional society is not limited only to constituted political authorities. Individuals are also involved in the abuse of power. I have selected at random the tale of the orphan girl to comment on how an individual who deviates from the community's norms of behavior meets with the wrath of the community and nemesis. The internal logic of the tale centres around the wanton use of power.

The Orphan Girl
Narrator: My story is about an orphan girl. Once upon a time, a man married two wives. The first one gave birth to a daughter and died soon after. Instead of giving the child to her mother's relations as tradition demands, the father decided to ignore tradition and gave the child to his second wife called Mangwi. Now Mangwi was a jealous and wicked woman. She was quick to notice that the child entrusted in her care whom we will call Shindoh was more intelligent than her own daughter, Ngwito. So she decided to make Shindoh do all the house work while Ngwito went out to play with her friends. One evening after a heavy rainfall, Mangwi decided to send Shindoh to the stream to wash the cooking utensils. Shindoh tried to complain that the stream was overflowing because of the heavy rains, but the stepmother would not listen. Rather she insisted that the poor orphan girl must go and wash the utensils. Shindoh left for the stream crying. In the process of washing the utensils, the fast flowing stream carried a bowl away. Shindoh knew immediately that she was in big trouble. Nevertheless, she hurried home and informed her stepmother. Mangwi was angry. She whipped Shindoh and drove her to go back to the stream and look for the missing bowl in spite of the fact that darkness was fast approaching. Left with no alternative, Shindoh went back to the stream and started following its course. Since it was already dark, Shindoh could not see well and soon slipped and fell into the fast flowing stream. She was swept away. But, to her surprise, she found herself in front of

an old woman's hut. The woman asked her how she found herself in front of the hut. Shindoh narrated her sad story. The old woman took pity of her and allowed her to spend the night in the hut on the condition that she swept the compound clean. Shindoh obeyed and after her chore, the old woman gave her food and showed her where to sleep.

The following day, she thanked the old woman for her generosity and got ready to continue her search for the missing bowl. The old woman asked her to go behind the house there she would find some eggs. Those eggs that shout "take me, take me", she should ignore. But she should take the egg that remained silent. She followed the instructions given to her and took the silent egg. The old woman then told her that when she got home she should enter her late mother's hut, close the door, and broke the egg. Once again she did as the old woman instructed. As soon as she broke the egg, several nice things including the missing bowl came out. She took the lost bowl to her stepmother and then invited everybody in the house to come and see her good fortune.

Instead of being happy, Mangwi became very jealous. She asked her own daughter, Ngwito to go to the stream and deliberately allow the stream to carry away one of the bowls and then she should follow the same itinerary as Shindoh. Ngwito did as she was instructed and eventually arrived at the old woman's hut. She was given the same chore by the old woman but she refused to obey. The old woman did not mind. When Ngwito was about to leave, the old woman instructed her to go behind the house where she would see some eggs. She should ignore those eggs that shout "take me, take me" and only take the silent one. When she went behind the house, she decided to take the first egg that shouted "take me, take me".

When she arrived home, she gathered her mother, father, and brothers in the house and closed the door leaving out Shindoh. But when she broke the egg, snakes, and all deadly diseases came out and wiped out the entire family. Only Shindoh survived, got married to a prince, and they lived happily thereafter. That is the end of my story (Recorded by K.I.Tala in Bamenda-Nkwe in 1985).

This is a story about the use and abuse of power. It is also about wickedness, greed, and graft. Thus, the action in the tale appropriately begins at home. In traditional Cameroon society, home is considered as a sanctuary in which peace, love and harmony prevail. When the story opens, Shindoh has just lost her mother. The death dislocates the normal family relationship existing in the home and creates a gap in the social and emotional life of the girl. The immediate issue at stake revolves around how to fill this gap. Tradition demands that under the circumstances, the girl should be placed in the care of her mother's people because they can better play the role of surrogate for her dead mother. The following wise saying taken form Chinua Achebe's *Things Fall Apart* (1958: 94), sheds more light on the issue: "It is true that a child belongs to its father. But when a father beats his child, it seeks sympathy in its mother's hut. A man belongs to his fatherland when things are good and life is sweet. But when there is sorrow and bitterness he finds refuge in his motherland".

The act of handing the girl over to her stepmother implies an overt transfer of power and the responsibility that goes with it. It is this power that Mangwi wantonly abuses. The main problem in the story can therefore be said to centre around the lack of restraint in the wielding of power. But power, as we all know, is dangerous in the sense that it is both corrupting and corruptible. That is why those who control it as is the case with Mangwi are expected by society to also recognize its obligatory moral nature. As Achebe reminds us in *Anthills of the Savannah* (1987:102)," in the beginning Power rampaged through our world, naked. So the Almighty decided to send his daughter, Idemili, to bear witness to the moral nature of authority by wrapping around Power's rude waist a loincloth of peace and modesty". The above passage is a warning against Mangwi's warped concept of behavior.

The pattern of human existence in traditional African society was coherent and at the same time contradictory. Although the society conducted its affairs on the basis of well-recognized positive values, so too was it materialistic. Achebe in (Ojinmah, 20) goes further to say that,

> *Anyone who has given thought to our society must be concerned by the brazen materialism one sees around. I have heard people blame it on Europe. That is utter rubbish. In fact the Nigerian society I know best – the Ibo society – has always been materialistic. This may sound strange because Ibo life had at the same time a strong spiritual dimension – controlled by gods, ancestors, personal spirits or chi and magic. The success of the culture was the balance between the two, the material and the spiritual.*

The implication of Achebe's observation is that the individual in Ibo society was called upon to balance the positive and negative values of his being. This is what Mangwi refuses to do. Rather, like Okonkwo in *Things Fall Apart,* she decides to treat Shindoh with a firmness that borders on callousness. Her deviation from the traditional norms of behavior is a flagrant disregard of the proverb, "if you bring up a child successfully in your youth, she will care for you at your old age". Furthermore, in the traditional world-view, once a child is placed in your care, that child becomes your child and must be treated as such. Hence the cautionary proverb, "a child's fingers are not scalded by a piece of hot yam which its mother puts in its palm". Thus, the insensitive stepmother, in total disregard of societal norms, not only creates disorder in the society but also arrogates unto herself the role of a superordinate, establishing and maintaining power in her relationship with her underling through the effective and continuous use of coercion, punishment and withdrawal of privileges.

The degree of Mangwi's qualmlessness and the margin of her deviation from normative structure becomes evident in the senseless act of sending Shindoh away at night in search of the missing bowl. That atrocious act of sending her away from the physical and spiritual protection of the home also marks the height of Mangwi's irresponsibility and the turning point of the story.

In the course of her perilous journey down the stream, Shindoh is exposed to the dangers of the hostile unfamiliar territory she is obliged to pass through. Her outward movement ends in front of the old woman's hut which serves as the "place of foreign sojourn" and which also marks the rite-of-passage phase. Her successful return with the egg which serves as a boon, is indicative of the victory of good over evil.

But, who is this venerable and marginalized old woman who lives on the fringes of society and yet succeeds in infiltrating it from the outside by saving helpless children like Shindoh from maltreatment and using them to restore justice and order in an unjust and disordered system? Isidore Okpewho (2000:8) attempts the following answer to the question.

> *In stories of this kind, the elements within the society sidelined by the configuration of power have a way of getting back at the system that has robbed them of their just deserts. The motif of an old woman who aids heroes in their quests has been acknowledged by folklorists as a universal folk narrative phenomenon.*

In the tale under study, the liminal old woman rescues Shindoh and prepares her for her eventual return to the village which is the centre of power as represented by Mangwi. Shindoh on her part, acquits herself honorably and is rewarded handsomely by the providential old woman. Shindoh returns home with an egg which turns out to be the boon with which she restores order and makes a positive difference in her society.

The figure of the old woman in this tale can thus be seen as a symbol of those who have been excluded from the circles of power but who have come back to haunt the autocratic system and teach it the basic ethical lesson that the people in power ill-treat or forget those they govern at their own peril.

Some scholars are of the opinion that orature serves exclusively to uphold the social structure and normative order. They are right to an extent because traditional institutions are sanctioned by checks and balances thereby making the extent of deviation from social norms very limited. That explains why there is hardly any serious challenge to constituted authority in that society. But, that should not be taken to mean that traditional institutions though desirable, are unquestionable. It does not also mean that because the oral artist lives in solidarity with his people and is close to his audience, he is therefore insensitive to matters of social conduct and of political probity. In fact, he often comments, counsels and observes on the past and the present. Seen from this perspective, orature becomes a social force and as such, naturally contains sentiments that are sometimes antagonistic to the ideology of the dominant social order.

I will now attempt to prove how orature's role as a source of ideological perception and criticism has been intensified as a result of the rapid social and political change which Cameroon has been undergoing since its initial exposure to the West. While social and political change in Europe assumed the form of a transition from an old traditional culture to a modern industrial one, the Cameroonian situation is more of a superimposition than a transition. As S. Biernaczky (1984:46) puts it, the Cameroonian society did not seem to have

> *experienced the clean break that the Western man often claims for his society between the concept and mode of thinking about life by unlettered representatives of a culture and the lettered ones that now seemed to dominate society. The cultures of the spoken and the written words as metaphors for traditional and modern civilizations have in the (Cameroonian) context been forced into heterosexual relationship, having had to share each other in spite of apparent differences in their anatomy.*

The co-existence of the old and the new cultures in contemporary Cameroon presupposes that orature has to cede some of its grounds to written literature and, as I have already pointed out, orature is losing the central position it once occupied in pre-literate society. Thus, the spread of literacy, the introduction of Christianity and a cash economy along with the rise of urban centres are all contributing in eroding the nutritive social contexts of orature.

If the impact of social and cultural change on Cameroon orature is minimal, it is more devastating on the traditional social philosophy of the people. As Achebe laments in an article in *African Writers Talking* (1975:13), " When two cultures meet, you would expect, if we were angels shall we say, we would pick out the best in the other and retain the best in our own, and this would be wonderful. But this doesn't happen often. What happens is that some of the worst elements of the old are retained and some of the worst of the new are added on to them".

It is therefore not surprising that society soon degenerates from a situation where the ideological assumptions of the people are sanctioned by the religious order and respected by the majority, to a situation where the normative order is so flagrantly abused by a privileged minority that it virtually ceases to exist.

So far, I have tried to establish the intricate relationship which exists between orature and social institutions in pre-colonial Cameroon. I have also highlighted the various functions which orature performs in that society. Finally, I made the point that the oral artist in traditional society, by the very nature of his profession, concerns himself with the state of his society. That explains why he is quick to notice that the dominant ideology of the constituted authority may not always be in harmony with the needs of the majority.

The oral artist, as I have shown, lives in a homogenous context and the worldview which he shares with his fellow villagers is circumscribed by the immediate cultural setting. Criticism, if there is any, is mainly at the private level. That is, the oral artist uses satire or innuendoes to castigate social deviants. When the need arises to call attention to the foibles or misdemeanor of the traditional authority, he does it through subtle allusions and, as a result, the ruler hardly takes offence. Thus, because of the peculiar nature of social relationships in pre-colonial Cameroon, it was neither necessary nor indeed desirable for orature to offer explicit contestation to the dominant ideology. Consequently, what was in common use was orature's implicit challenge to the social order. The genres best suited for these regulatory tasks were the oral tales, proverbs and folk songs.

Generally speaking then, orature served as an instrument for the examination of individual experience in relation to the normative order of society. It was also used to comment on how the individual adheres to or deviates from the community's norms of behavior.

So far, I have underlined the didactic proportions of orature in order to demonstrate aspects of our past which we can use today to prepare for tomorrow.

A Brief Historical Background
Historically, French Cameroun was granted political independence by France on 1st January 1960 and became La Republique du Cameroun with Ahmadou Ahidjo as its first President. After the Plebiscite organized by the United Nations on 11 February, 1961, British Southern Cameroons voted to achieve political independence by reuniting with La Republique du Cameroun.

A Constitutional Conference was convened in July, 1961 in Foumban to allow the two parties – La Republique du Cameroun and British Southern Cameroons – to finalize arrangements for their political re-union. On 1st October, 1961, the Federal Republic of Cameroon officially came into being.

Anglophone intellectuals were among the first to question the concept of a re-union. Carlson Anyangwe in (Ngeh, 74) argued that what took place was more of a union than a re-union.

> *If the Southern Cameroons were ever a part of La Republique du Cameroun, then there would have been no necessity for the 1961 invitation to the Southern Cameroons to achieve independence by joining Republique du Cameroun. The Southern Cameroons would simply have been transferred to Republique du Cameroun like Hong Kong to China. Southern Cameroons' independence by joining Republique du Cameroun led to the disappearance or submergence of the respective international personalities of the Southern Cameroons and Republique du Cameroun... Republique du Cameroun's so called historic right over the Southern Cameroons is an extremely absurd, idle, frivolous and vexatious claim indefensible in neither international nor municipal law.*

Thomas Ngomba Ekali in (Ngeh, 67-68) on his part, expressed strong doubts about the appropriateness of the Federal System.

> *The establishment and operation of a Federal system of government between the Republic of Cameroon which became East Cameroon, and the Southern Cameroons which became West Cameroon was bound to be different in both states. This was dictated by the differences in their political traditions and cultures. While West Cameroonians hoped for the establishment of a loose federation with more powers to the states and reduced powers to the Central Government, East Cameroonians were lukewarm to the idea of a federation which was the antithesis of the political system under which they had been groomed.*

Ironically, President Ahidjo who ardently championed the cause of the Federal System, and took pains to assure the Anglophone leaders that the interests of the Anglophones would be safeguarded, was the first to turn around and campaign for its demise on grounds that it was too expensive to run. As Victor Julius Ngoh (2004:144) points out,

> *The Cameroon federation was, according to Ahidjo too expensive for Cameroon. Cameroonians, in his view, had to bear the burden of financing four assemblies, namely: the Federal Assembly, the East Cameroon Assembly, the West Cameroon Assembly and the West Cameroon House of Chiefs. The Cameroonian people also had to finance three governments, namely, the Federal, East Cameroon and West Cameroon Governments. The corollary was the expensive duplication of services. The end result was that the cost of maintaining the Federal system drained the country's coffers of billions of francs CFA which Ahidjo argued could be more properly used for the economic, cultural and social development of the entire country.*

Ahidjo's argument was both logical and plausible from the point of view of economics even though it was in flagrant violation of the Foumban Constitution. Accordingly, a Referandum was organized on 20 May, 1972 which led to the transformation of the country from a Federal State to a Unitary State. Bernard Fonlon, The eminent Cameroonian philosopher and personal friend of Ahidjo in (Ngeh, 73), was quick to see through Ahidjo's hidden agenda and sounded the following warning:

> *Unless the East Cameroon leader and intellectual, in whose hands cultural initiative lies, is prepared to share this authority with his brother from West of the Mungo, unless he is prepared to make the giant effort necessary to break loose from the strait-jacket of his French education, unless he will show proof of his intellectual probity and admit candidly that there are things in the Anglo-Saxon way of life that can do his country good, there is little chance of survival, neither for English influence, nor even for African values in the Federal Republic of Cameroon. With African culture moribund, with John Bullism weak and in danger of being smothered, we will all be French in two decades or three.*

Between 1961 and 1972, Ahidjo confronted two major obstacles to the consolidation of his dictatorial power: virulent opposition from the UPC and the problem of integrating Anglophone West Cameroon into the centralized system of governance. His astute political sense enabled him to overcome both obstacles but the problems they caused have left indelible scars on the political life of Cameroon. As Willibroad Dze-Ngwa (2008:130) submits,

> *Political evolution in the country saw the disrespect of the union accords by Francophone dominated governments. This made it easy for the political, economic and socio-cultural domination and marginalization of Anglophone Cameroonians who constituted a minority in the union, resulting in what became known as the "Anglophone Problem". This problem led to an increasing spirit of Anglophone nationalism and mutual suspicion between Anglophone and Francophone dichotomy in the political, economic and socio-cultural domains.*

Ahidjo's myth of National Unity which was the fulcrum of his national integration policy became, in the long run, as Fonlon has prophesied, a subterfuge for subjugating, oppressing and assimilating Anglophone Cameroonians. The mythology surrounding his person and his nation-building rhetoric also contributed in obscuring the increasing centralization of decision-making power at the Presidency and the consolidation of a comprador class. The spineless members of that privileged class, by aligning themselves with the autocratic Ahidjo, were able to turn a blind eye to the corruption around them, condone the excesses they see and become themselves puppets in the hands of puppeteers. As a result, they saw governance as a matter of how long they were able to cling to power. It could therefore be said that in economic terms, Cameroon enjoyed growing prosperity under Ahidjo's autocratic rule. Nevertheless, beneath that apparent success there were serious imbalances in the country's cultural, political and social life.

    The attainment of political independence by Cameroon in 1960 it will be recalled, generated the promise of a better future for the ethnically diverse country. Cameroonians took pride in their new nation and expected conditions to improve. They were motivated by President Ahmadou Ahidjo's official rhetoric which revolved around the lofty idea of a Cameroon that would be unified, productive, and confident of its own identity. But, as Richard Bjornson (458) points out,

> *When the Ahidjo government consolidated its power after independence, it acted in the belief that the new national identity could be forged by a ruling elite and imposed on the people from above. At the same time, it promoted an alternative utopian vision based on unity, development, cultural nationalism, and discipline. In reality, the society that emerged under Ahidjo contrasted sharply with this utopian vision, and popular disillusionment with the promise of independence became a dominant theme in the writings of postcolonial Cameroonian writers.*

Ahidjo also propagated an ethnically based patronage system which disregarded the respect for competence, the sense of civic responsibility and the work ethic. His government encouraged a privileged minority to monopolize wealth, power and status while the majority of their fellow countrymen were mired in abject poverty. Thus, while Ahidjo was promising a comfortable life for Cameroonians, his government was doing everything possible to undermine those things that would have made that better life possible. Bjornson (111) points out that as a result of Ahidjo's management style, the privileged class in Cameroon, appropriated a disproportionate share of the country's wealth.

> By the early 1970s, less than two percent of the total population received a third of the national income; the next ten percent also received a third, leaving the final third to be distributed among more than eighty percent of the population. This gap in income distribution becomes even wider when one considers the other prerequisites reserved for the privileged class - subsidized housing, access to better medical care, admission to elite public schools for their children, and the expediting of administrative decisions.

Thus, Ahidjo used his official rhetoric as a convenient means of camouflaging the gross imbalance in the distribution of national income and other social ills. He also used two political instruments to tighten his stranglehold on Cameroonians - the constitution which gave him autocratic powers and the single-party system which was used to brainwash the masses to accept without question whatever they were told by the Party.

But, the enlightened dictator, Ahidjo also had his "heels of Achilles" which was the "Pacte Colonial" which he signed with France as a precondition for the granting of political independence in 1960 and which inevitably locked Cameroon into the economic and military embrace of France. This obnoxious Agreement signed between France and Cameroon according to Gary K. Busch (2011:3), "not only created the institution of the CFA franc, it created a legal mechanism under which France obtained a special place in the political and economic life of Cameroon". In fact, France coerced all the Presidents of her newly liberated African colonies to sign the infamous "Pacte Colonial" and, as Busch (4) avers,

> The colonial pact maintained the French control over the economies of the African states; it took possession of their foreign currency reserves; it controlled the strategic raw materials of the country; it stationed troops in the country with the right of free passage; it

> *demanded that all military equipment be acquired from France; it took over the training of the police and army; it required that French businesses be allowed to maintain monopoly enterprises in key areas (water, electricity, ports, transport, energy, etc.). France not only set limits on the imports of a range of items from outside the franc zone but also set minimum quantities of imports from France. These treaties are still in force and operational.*

The consequences for Cameroon of the continuation of a policy of total dependence on France was obvious – "lack of competitive options; dependence on the French economy; dependence on the French military; and the open-door policy for French private enterprise". For instance, French firms virtually controlled all the business sectors in Cameroon: Bollore, Saga, and Delmas (maritime transport and the port of Douala); Bouygues (construction and public works); Total (petrol stations); France Telecom (telecommunication); Societe General, Credit Lyonnais and BNP-Paribas (banking and insurance). Thus, France surreptitiously dictated Cameroon's foreign policy, controlled most of the infrastructure and maintained a stranglehold on the country's commerce and currency, all of which vitiated national initiative towards meaningful independence. It is regrettable to note that in spite of the devastating effects of the "Pacte Colonial" on the long suffering Cameroonians, Ahidjo never contemplated renouncing that agreement. Furthermore, the massive presence of the French in Cameroon ensured the dominance of the French language, French tastes and French modes of thought. It is worth noting that the French created the dreaded secret police which became the distinctive feature of the Ahidjo regime.

    The Cameroonian Constitution under Ahidjo provided for certain "inalienable and sacred rights", including "the freedom of communication, of expression of the press, of assembly (and) of association". However that was in principle only. In practice, the government regularly restricted these rights. It interfered with the media, and harassed all those who expressed views at odds with government policy.

Under the circumstances, the construction of protest discourse in the 1960s and 1970s became a very dangerous undertaking in Cameroon as freedom of expression was systematically stifled by the oppressive Ahidjo regime. Journalists, who tried to protest against the repressive and coercive tendencies of the political authority, were arbitrarily detained and tortured. The few critical administrative elite who refused to be muzzled were summarily jailed. The radio which was the most important medium for disseminating information in the country became a sensitive political channel and presenters were careful to avoid any political representation that could be interpreted as an attack on the authoritative regime. Discontented and disillusioned creative writers like Mongo Beti, Rene Philombe, Benjamin Matip, and Patrice Ndedi Penda who criticized the Ahidjo government for condoning widespread corruption, favouritism, hypocrisy and the conspicuous consumption of the privileged class were either imprisoned, forced into exile, or were subjected to various forms of harassment.

Under such draconian conditions of fear and apprehension perpetrated by the totalitarian regime, the powerless and voiceless masses were constrained to choose the path of least resistance. They handed over critical comment to the oral artist whom they saw as a sociopolitical commentator and their outspoken voice. That action of the exploited and oppressed masses is understandable and is based on the old adage that a public starved of critical self-expression would normally look for appropriate public icons in which to anchor their repressed emotions.

A momentous political and historical change took place in Cameroon on 6 November, 1982 when President Ahidjo suddenly and unilaterally decided to hand over political power to his Prime Minister, Paul Biya. As was to be expected, when Biya assumed power, he immediately distanced himself from Ahidjo and his authoritarian patterns of governance. He projected himself as a man of the people. He caught public attention as a crusader of civic responsibility. His key slogan was "moral renewal". Hence, his recognition of the need to eliminate corruption, inequitable distribution of wealth, and arbitrary restrictions on freedom of expression endeared him to Cameroonians especially the disaffected and disgruntled Anglophone population.

Biya's democratic inclinations and his utopian impetus towards freedom of expression were incorporated in his *Pour le liberalism Communautaire* (Communal Liberalism). In that seminal book, Biya revealed his liberal democratic vision for the country, and promised a "charter of freedom" that will lead to the emergence of an emancipated Cameroon. As he himself declares in (Bjorson,286), "it is necessary to create in every Cameroonian the conditions of a national consciousness so profound that primary, instinctive attachments to tribal or regional values and interests can no longer disturb it".

Biya's political reign has had its ups and downs and its twists and turns. Apart from the attempted coup of 6 April, 1984, several other major incidents have marked Biya's reign and also helped to undermine his good intentions and reform programmes. The political atmosphere and the economic situation worsened again and the country began to experience a major economic downturn. As Bjornson (284) observed,

> *Corruption and mismanagement contributed directly to the worsening economic situation. Smuggling, overbilling, payment for development projects that were never realized, and the skimming of percentages from government contracts cost the federal treasury billions of cfa francs, with the fall of oil and raw material prices, Cameroon had become a debtor nation by the late 1980s.*

On the international scene, there were the liberalization exigencies of the Bretton Woods institutions, the German reunification, and the collapse of the Soviet Union among other pressures which set in motion a wind of democratic change which swept through the African continent and ushered in a new political era in Cameroon governed by the rule of law. Nyamnjoh (113) summarizes the situation as follows:

> *With the Eastern European revolution in 1989, disaffected Cameroonians in their numbers felt that the time has come to quench a thirst long ignored: the thirst*

to be liberated from dictatorial complacencies, endemic corruption and suffocating mediocrity. They were fed up with power-mad dictators hiding behind the nebulous notions of national development and stability to disarm all forms of opposition. Everyone had come to know that such stability was phoney and development elusive. They wanted change – multi-party democracy, with the hope that this would bring about pluralism and popular democratic participation in practice. Mono-partism made large promises for Cameroon, but failed to deliver even the meanest minimum. Their argument was that if thirty years of sacrificed freedom were not time enough to have attained the promised land of unity, integration and betterment for all and sundry, then mono-partism was a problem not a solution.

By the early nineties however, Cameroon was already in deep economic crisis. Unemployment was high especially among the educated youth. The majority of Cameroonians were living in abject poverty and the prospects for a better tomorrow were bleak. It was at this inauspicious moment that the wind of democratic change mentioned above, blew over Cameroon and ushered in the era of multipartism. The Social Democratic Front Party (SDF) which was founded in Bamenda in 1990 easily became the strongest opposition party in the country. It contested the Presidential elections of 1992 with the ruling Cameroon People's Democratic Movement (CPDM). The conduct of the elections was controversial and provoked an acrimonious row which made bitter enemies of all the parties concerned. The SDF accused the CPDM of rigging the elections and of stealing their hard-earned victory. In order to break the ensuing deadlock, the opposition parties decided to exploit the naivety of the youths by encouraging them to make several forays into CPDM territory. The social tension generated by the events soon degenerated into the infamous Ghost Town. The events were quick to take a dramatic turn for the worse as the hitherto docile youths became riotous and went on the rampage. They burnt tyres on roads, erected barricades at random, introduced the dreadful "red card", and extorted arbitrary toll from road users. Those who hesitated to pay or did not carry enough money on them were molested and humiliated. The youngsters imposed their own curfew, looted shops and destroyed life and property. In short, they held the whole country hostage for months on end. That heralded the beginning of civil disobedience and the gross disregard for constituted authority which has become endemic in Cameroon.

Another incident is the social upheavals of February, 2008. It all started as a simple nation-wide strike organized by public transporters ostensibly to protest against high fuel cost. But, before the government could react, the restive youths who had their own grievances against the state, seized the initiative and plunged the country into a season of anomy. Large groups of angry youth protested in the streets of Yaounde, Douala, Bamenda, and other major towns throughout the country. They looted shops and vandalized property. In short, they paralyzed the nation for close to one week by virtually re-enacting the Ghost Town scenario.

Until the end of the 1990s therefore, the Cameroonian political landscape was in perpetual tumult. Corruption was still endemic in the society. The economy was still firmly controlled by the West and the country was still groaning under the weight of a heavy debt burden. The gap between the affluent minority and the indigent majority was widening. In short growth and modernization were still being stultified by tribalism, favouritism and nepotism.

Confronted by the above problems over which he had very little control, Biya chose the path of least resistance and resorted to the Machiavellian machinations of his astute predecessor. Censorship was reintroduced and applied with the utmost rigour. The early champions for the cause of political liberalism and multi-party democracy like Yondo Black, Pius Njawe, Celestin Monga and Ni John Fru Ndi were arbitrarily arrested, detained, brutalized, and even imprisoned.

But, from the early 2000, things began to take a turn for the better. Cameroonians are now enjoying a certain degree of freedom of expression. The private media is flourishing. Multipartism has become a reality and concerted efforts are being made to guarantee free and fair elections. The government is waging a relentless war against corruption, and is also working hard to ensure good governance. Finally, the government has launched a massive recruitment drive especially among the educated youths. In spite of these and other laudable advances in democracy and good governance however, much still remain to be done. It is hoped that the government will not rest on its laurels.

Therefore, unlike the traditional society which was largely homogenous, collectivist, and cooperative, the contemporary Cameroonian society is individualistic, heterogeneous, and multicultural. It is normless and has no specific expectations from its members. Consequently, the oral artist now finds that he has to transcend his immediate cultural environment to embrace the new and nebulous concept of a Cameroonian nation. He discovers that relationships among individuals are being controlled by the cash nexus. It also dawns on him that the reorganization of social, economic and political relationship in the modern context is adversely affecting the traditional lifestyles which sustain orature.

Furthermore, he finds that the disregard for the normative order has moved from a "micro: interpersonal level to a macro: individual versus community basis". All these discoveries lead him to the conclusion that his oral texts must evolve with time, place, and audience. Also the style and content of the orature have to change as the values and conditions of his country change. That is as it should be. For, as Ngara (29) puts it,

> The dynamics of political struggles and social change affect the content and form of works of art so that if we are to understand fully and appreciate the rise, development, concerns and styles of the literature of a nation we must see that literature in relation to the history and struggles of its people, and in relation to the various ideologies that issue from socio-economic conditions.

Ngara's assertion confirms the fact that orature is not static or unchanging. In other words, the change in the form and content of orature is caused by the social and political mutation which the society is undergoing. This position is further bolstered by Ropo Sekoni's contention in (Bernaczky: 147) that,

> *Since the issue of individual – community dialectic seems to be an ever-present one in human affairs, the ideological role of literature as an indirect socialization of the individual to the dynamics... of cultural practice, often a source of inspiration and organization for oral narratives, may be a model for aesthetic discourse on social practice... The modern audience, like its traditional counterparts, deserve to know the difference between negative and positive challenges of community norms.*

In postcolonial Cameroon then, orature and politics have become interwoven to the extent that the oral literary artist has become more visible on the political scene and is being used by those who exercise power and those who are recipients of the exercise of power. Finnegan in (Kaschula, xiii), pointed out some time ago that forms of orature "are now accepted by African political parties as a vehicle for communication, propaganda political pressure, and political education … As such they are a powerful and flexible weapon in many types of political activity" Charismatic African leaders such as Kwame Nkrumah of Ghana, Jomo Kenyatta of Kenya, Kenneth Kaunda of Zambia, Kamazu Banda of Malawi and Ahmadou Ahidjo of Cameroon have taken advantage of orature as a communication strategy because it enabled their people to understand them. Campton (317) concerns himself with the use of the oral literary artists as socio-political orators by socialist governments.

> *Socialist governments have tended to emphasize and make use of folk media for political education and nation building to a much greater extent – and in a more coherent 'policy and program' fashion – than have many governments of non-socialist countries. Extensive and effective use has been made of indigenous troupes of folk art performance in mass campaigns to propagate ideology and motivate rural people in several countries in Asia, Africa, and Latin America.*

It is clear from the above that orature is being used and manipulated as part of political rhetoric by people on both sides of the political divide. However, my focus in this book is not so much on the privileged minority who have monopolized wealth, power and status. Rather, it is on the impoverished and marginalized Cameroonians who are struggling for survival. I am interested in their exploitation of the contestative nature of their orature. But, before delving into that, it may be necessary for me to examine, however briefly, the effectiveness of orature as a vehicle of protest and defiance.

The critical ideological possibilities of orature has long been acknowledged by scholars. For the Italian Marxist Sociologist, Luigi Lombardi-Satriani in (J.E. Limon, 1985:156) orature, as folklore,

> ... *actively contests the hegemony of dominant social orders and it does so in two modes. First, folklore has the capacity for direct contestation. That is, it can directly symbolize and 'name' the class enemy in the manner of political jokes and protest songs. However, and of greater interest, we are also told that folklore can also offer direct contestation by its presence. That is, subordinate classes produce a number of autonomous behaviours (largely in the generic realms of ritual and material culture) whose very existence limits the total hegemony of parallel products and behaviours emanating from the dominant social order.*

Thus, for Lombardi-Satriani, orature plays a vital role as "counter hegemonic activity". That is, it attacks individuals, communities or institutions who violate the traditional norms.

Like Lombardi-Satriani, William Fox in (Limon, 47), also recognizes orature's capacity for direct and indirect contestation. But, unlike Lombardi-Satriani who attributes the oppositional quality of orature to "its presence", Fox believes that the contestative nature can be found in orature's "ability to accumulate and assert, often by metaphor and analogy, both past injustices and hopes and aspirations left unfulfilled by the social order" . He concludes by positing that orature "strengthens the internal cohesion of a group and thereby maximizes its solidarity and survival against a dominant order"

Raymond Williams in (Limon, 48), echoes both Lombardi-Satriani and Fox when he asserts that orature actively contests the hegemony of dominant social orders. However, he departs somehow from them when he claims that orature is inherently critical because "it represents areas of human experience and aspiration, and achievement which the dominant culture neglects, undervalues, opposes, represses, or even cannot recognize".

Finally, Herbert Marcuse in (Limon, 38), endorses the views of the earlier thinkers that orature is inherently emancipatory but disagrees with them on the modality of emancipation. For him, orature is art and art is "committed to an emancipation of sensibility, imagination, and reason in all spheres of subjectivity and objectivity… it becomes a vehicle of recognition and indictment".

For each of these thinkers, orature has obvious critical ideological possibilities. That is, it can challenge the social order directly or indirectly. However, while these scholars present orature as an inherently critical force and are optimistic about its continuity in the contemporary world, there is another school of thought which is less optimistic about the prospects of orature and, consequently, its critical ideological possibilities. According to this pessimistic group of scholars, orature has only a "marginal and problematic existence" in the contemporary world. For example, the literary critic Fredric Jameson in (Limon, 40), observes that:

> *The popular and folk arts reflected and were dependent for their production on quite different social realities. They were the organic expression of so many distinct social communities or castes, such as the peasant village, the court, the medieval town, the polis, and even the classical bourgeoisie when it was still a unified social group with its own cultural specificity. Advanced capitalism, however, has induced folklore's decline, not by attacking the expression itself but by dissolving, fragmenting, and anatomizing its nutritive social contexts by way of the corrosive action of universal commodification and the market system.*

For Jameson, then, "the reorganization of society in advanced capitalism has led to the erosion of those social groupings that sustained" orature. Put differently, Jameson confines orature to history and the museum. Another scholar who sees orature as a largely historical and antiquarian phenomenon is Walter Benjamin in (Limon, 39). According to him,

> The art of storytelling is coming to an end. Less and less frequently do we encounter people with the ability to tell a tale properly ... it is as if something that seemed inalienable to us, the securest among our possessions, were taken from us: the ability to exchange experiences. The face to face milieu of craft production nurtured storytelling, but today it is becoming unraveled at all of its ends after being woven thousands of years ago in the ambiance of the oldest forms of craftsmanship.

These scholars tend to see orature as a fossilized form of a primitive past. They give the impression that even if orature manages to exist in contemporary contexts, it will be under very marginalized conditions. But what these scholars fail to understand is that the very forces militating against the continued existence of orature are the very forces that are ironically ensuring its continuity. Furthermore, because the texts of orature are oral, they can neither be static nor unchanging. Thus, the texts are likely to evolve with time, place, performer and audience in other to keep the ideas relevant. This position is shared by Finnegan in (Kaschula, 281), when she states that:

> The trend now is certainly away from the older dismissal of oral forms as necessarily something of the past, into an awareness of how a whole range of interacting media (oral, written, electronic) are now readily used for a wide variety of contemporary purposes as a normal part of modern life.

I have demonstrated in this chapter that there is indeed a vital role for orature in Cameroon today. I have also shown that it has the potential for use as a powerful medium for political activism. In the next chapter, I will focus on its use for educational purposes.

CHAPTER TWO
ORATURE AND ETHOLOGICAL EDUCATION

> *If we honestly and critically examine our so called modern society today, we will arrive at an incontrovertible and; more importantly, accurate conclusion: virtually every facet of our national life has either disintegrated or collapsed. Indeed, we can justifiably say it is desperately in need of mending. The mad greed for great gain in our youth is well known, the profundity of corruption and prominence of graft in our public life (even at government level), the high level of disregard, infact contempt for discipline and decorum, completes the excellent portrait of the Augean stables called our country* (Nkem Okoh, 2008:223).

The purpose of this chapter is to stimulate and contribute to action-oriented debate relating to the fundamental problem facing educationists in Cameroon. That problem, put quite simply, is the rapid and significant decline in the ethological aspects of the education offered in Cameroon since the attainment of political independence. The resulting moral depravity became all the more pernicious because it has, in turn, engendered such insidious evils as corruption, embezzlement, kleptomania, unbridled materialism, and the personalization and monopolization of power.

This dehumanizing and gangrenous phenomenon has raised compelling issues with questions that require urgent answers. One of these issues is the relevance and adequacy of the present education system in Cameroon. As C.J. Brumfit and R.A. Carter (1986: 223) have questioned, "What is the philosophy behind it? What are its guidelines? What and whose social vision is it setting out to serve? The obvious answer to these questions are that the educational system originated from imperialist Europe. It was managed in the first instance by the Europeans themselves and later by their Cameroonian surrogates for the purposes of imperialist domination and cultural oppression. The implication here is that the education system has been designed to serve the exclusive interests of the West in contradistinction with the interests of Cameroonians. That explains why it undermines the traditional ideological matrix of collective solidarity and collective responsibility. It also explains why colonial education undermines the teaching of orature in Cameroonian schools. That is to be expected because there is no such thing as a natural education process. Richard Shaull in the "Foreword" to Paulo Freire's seminal book, Pedagogy of the Oppressed (1982: 15) confirms this when he declares that:

> *Education either functions as an instrument which is used to facilitate the integration of the younger generation into the logic of the present system and bring about conformity to it, or it becomes "the practice of freedom" by which men and women deal critically and creatively with reality and discover how to participate in the transformation of their world.*

In the colonial and postcolonial contexts, it is the former option that has prevailed and is still prevailing. Freire (71), identifies two concepts of education – the Banking and the Problem-posing. The former inhibits the creative power of the individual while the latter encourages it. That, according to Freire, explains why the two concepts and practices come into conflict:

> *Banking education (for obvious reasons) attempts, by mythicizing reality, to conceal certain facts which explain the way men exist in the world; problem-posing education sets itself the task of demythologizing. Banking education resists dialogue; problem-posing education regards dialogue as indispensable to the act of cognition which unveils reality. Banking education treats students as objects of assistance; problem-posing education makes them critical thinkers. Banking education inhibits creativity and domesticate (although it cannot completely destroy) the intentionality of consciousness by isolating consciousness from the world, thereby denying men their ontological and historical vocation of becoming more fully human. Problem-posing education bases itself on creativity and stimulates true reflection and action upon reality,*

> *thereby responding to the vocation of men as beings who are authentic only when engaged in inquiry and creative transformation. In sum: banking theory and practice, as immobilizing and fixating forces, fail to acknowledge men as historical beings; problem-posing theory and practice take man's historicity as their starting point.*

It is from this standpoint therefore, that I want to posit that the moral decadence in our body politic today is the result of the European imperialist bourgeois philosophy behind the educational system bequeathed to us by our erstwhile colonial masters and the paucity of the ethical and moral content of the western literature that is being taught in our schools. This position has been corroborated by Fonlon (1965: 19) when he lamented the debilitating impact of the individual experience which is the product of the devious and invidious colonial educational system:

> *Under colonial government the new education is reserved for the few; and to the few it is not manly courage and value that are held up as ideals worthy of their pursuit. No, rather it is pleasure; it is the hoarding of wealth, of money, as the surest way to pleasure. And colonial conquerors have always known that there is hardly a means more insidious, more infallible of emptying a people of manliness and making them willing slaves than to excite, especially in their elite and leadership, an insatiable thirst for pleasure.*

Individualism then, is the product of the sinister and maleficent educational system which we inherited at independence and which has given birth to a flagrant disregard of the necessary moralities of human intercourse, to political chicanery and to a protocol of thieving which have virtually ruined the very vitals of our society. This point is further reinforced by Vaughan in (Gugelberger, 218):

> *The educational system itself – a condition of access to petty bourgeois status – becomes highly suspect, since it appears to exist only to fill places within the present set-up, and to foster the individualism and elitism of a select minority. The condition of the vast majority of the people will not be changed by the educational system,*

since education is not necessary to the labour functions that the majority performs.

Thus, not only do we need a radical reversal, we also need a new educational system which will incorporate the indigenous knowledge embedded in our orature. In other words, we need a "problem-posing education" system. Such an action is salutary because orature, as J.G.W. Ahukana in (Ako, 1996:310) declares, is one of the most powerful tools that an educational system can use to "inculcate values, develop skills, influence attitude and affect physical, social, emotional, intellectual and moral development".

Before delving into the heart of the matter however, it may be necessary for me to define the term "education". Generally speaking, education is the process of establishing habits of critical thinking, intellectual development and independent appraisal of human values and qualities. Fonlon (1965: 15) defines education in a similar vein as "the physical, the aesthetic, the intellectual and the moral upbringing of a man". Seen from this perspective, education is meant to develop the individual intellectually and morally, and prepare him to function effectively in society. Unfortunately, the present educational system which is based on the "banking concept," is not geared towards that goal. Furthermore, the impact of the western literary culture on our orature has been negative.

Fonlon (14) goes further to state that if education is to perform its fundamental function of nurturing the individual, it must, of necessity have a system. The nature of this system of education, according to him,

> *Will depend, in the main on what sort of individual that particular society wants to produce, on what is their idea of the perfect man. And their idea of the perfect man will depend, to a large extent, on the problems that beset the society; for their ideal man will be the man best equipped, best able to meet these problems.*

Thus, Fonlon is saying that an educational system is established by a particular society to meet its specific needs. J.B. Agbase (2000: 54) reinforces Fonlon's point when he affirms that:

> *No educational system stands apart from the society which establishes it. It has purposes that must be achieved if that society is to continue in the right direction. Education is meant to be embedded in that society, drawing inspiration and nourishment from it, and in turn contributing to societal opportunities for growth and renewal.*

The present educational system in Cameroon does not fulfill the conditions outlined by Agbase in the above excerpt. That explains in part why it concentrates on imparting cognitive, linguistic and vocational skills which transform young Cameroonians into efficient machines designed exclusively for the labour market. At the same time, it ignores the teaching of indigenous knowledge and humanistic values contained in the orature which help in the creation of socially responsible individuals. Since the Educational system was not designed specifically for Cameroonians, it follows, logically that there is an urgent need to reorientate and relate it to the rehabilitation of Cameroon's culture, tradition and value systems.

The point must be made here and strongly too that before the advent of colonialism, Cameroonians like other Africans had a viable traditional educational system. It was informal. That is, through watching and imitating the examples of grown-ups and by participating in the daily life of the community. Cultural content and cultural behavior were passed on to the young through orature. Austin Bukenya (1994: 2) propounds on the educational relevance of orature in the following excerpt:

> *I believe we undertake it mainly because we are convinced that it is a valuable educational experience contributing to the total growth, development and self-fulfillment of the person exposed to it. Oral literature imparts to the growing person useful cognitive and affective skills which enable the person to live a rewarding life and to be a useful member of the society. Oral literature should make the learner more keenly observant, more sensibly and sensitively responsive towards her or his own self, fellow human beings and the environment. Above all, oral literature being a mode of communication should make the learner a competent,*

> *more skilful and more concerned communicator, especially through the oral mode.*

Donna Rosenberg (1996 : xxvi) on her part, is concerned with the moral capacity of orature to help members of a community to make sense out of nonsense and to create order out of chaos by providing moral answers to such philosophical questions as:

> *Who am I? What is the nature of the universe in which I live? How do I relate to both the known and the unknown world? How much control do I have over my own life? What must I do to survive? How can I balance my own desires with my responsibilities to my family, my community, and the powers that control my world? How can I reconcile myself to the inevitability of death?*

Thus, by deliberately refusing to incorporate orature fully into the educational system, the colonial administrators were promoting their imperial interests; and, by encouraging the Cameroonian government to continue to neglect the teaching of orature in the schools, the neo-colonialists were indirectly asking Cameroonians to commit cultural suicide. This view is upheld by a World Bank Report (2007: 12) on "Development and the Next Generation "which states that:

> *There are practical things in life that secondary school doesn't even touch upon, for example, how to confront and solve problems which are more adequately handled by our folklore and indigenous knowledge systems. When young people are introduced to logical and critical reflections on difficult situations as through our orature, they normally grow to cultivate a habit of resolving difficult economic and sociopolitical problems with relative ease.*

Therefore, after over five decades of political independence, our orature is yet to be fully integrated into the Cameroon education system. In other words, our Government either through ignorance or the servile attachment to other people's values to the detriment of our own, is yet to adapt the colonial education system that we inherited to the reality of the Cameroonian situation. Hence, the serious incongruities which exist between what is being taught in our schools, colleges, and universities today, and what is socially and politically relevant.

The Educational System and National Development
The Cameroon educational system is currently being managed by three ministries: the Ministry of Basic Education, the Ministry of Secondary Education, and the Ministry of Higher Education. These three ministries have as mandate to ensure the provision of quality education to Cameroonian youths who will, in turn, contribute to national development. This very heavy responsibility implies among other things that the educational system should be designed in such a way as to accommodate all levels of student ability and all areas of interest. To facilitate the task of these ministries, the Government has, over the years, been allocating a significant portion of its national budget to this sector. But the end results have been far from satisfactory. Several factors have contributed to bringing the problems of education to a head especially at the tertiary level. To begin with, the education system itself is a carryover from the colonial era and therefore is not tailored to meet the changing needs of the nation and of the global economy. Budgetary allocation to the state universities are both in- adequate and irregular. The student-teacher ratio is constantly on the rise. The learning process is still teacher centred with the blackboard and chalk being the main teaching aids. Lectures form the bulk of the teaching process. Tutorials, though important, hardly hold because of lack of space. When they manage to hold, they are ineffective because the groups are too large. Because of the size of the classes, it is difficult to encourage students to seek information for themselves by carrying out assignments. Thus, hand-outs from lecturers form the major source of information. As a consequence of the University Reforms of 1993, computer lessons have been introduced. But that is in theory only. In practice, the classes are not effective because there is one computer to about five hundred students. Both theoretical and practical research are yet to receive the attention they deserve from the state. Another serious problem is that of inadequate infrastructure. For example, the teaching staff

has difficulties in finding office space for receiving students, for preparing lectures or for marking scripts. Efforts are being made to increase the number of academic staff, but the increase is not keeping pace with that of the students. There is no staff development programmes for the teaching and support staff, and sabbaticals remain a dream.

Most of the students are from peasant background. They feel that engaging in agricultural activities will leave them at the same social level as their parents. Hence, their obsession with the obtention of a university degree. They tend to lose sight of the fact that a university degree is not an end in itself. They also fail to realize that what they actually need to acquire are the knowledge and skills necessary to secure employment that provide income that is sufficient to live comfortably.

By 1982, the Cameroonian economy began its downturn. The income derived from petrol which would have helped to cushion the continuing economic down-swing belonged largely to such multinational petroleum companies as ELF and Total. What was supposed to be Cameroon's share was diverted by the political leadership. The market price of Cameroonian raw material: coffee, cocoa, banana, cotton, rubber, and timber also took a nose-dive. The reduced national income meant that the Government could no longer meet all its financial obligations. It also meant that the state could no longer continue to recruit graduates into the civil service. The slump in the job market for graduates in turn, demotivated students.

The Cameroon Government is, of course, fully aware of its obligation to give access to as many Cameroonians as possible to as much education as possible. That is why it has put in place short term and long term measures to stem the rapid increase in the population of the educated unemployed. These include the re-training of graduates from the faculties of Arts and Law to give them practical and marketable skills to enable them find employment. There is also a reassessment of the objectives of higher education institutions with emphasis on profession-oriented courses. But, these and other measures though laudable, are grossly inadequate. Thus, unemployment, especially among the educated youths, continue to rise. The frustration among the educated unemployed is further aggravated by the fact that recruitment into the few available openings is no longer based on what you know but on whom you know and the amount of money in your pocket.

The rising number of educated and less educated youths have led to the devaluation of academic qualifications and an increase in the rate of attrition in the country. As a result, Cameroonian youths have been forced to turn to the informal sector for alternative employment. Indeed, it is this devaluation of academic qualifications and the pauperization of the unemployed youths that irk the protest musicians. This is the subject of Lapiro's album, "Na You, Ndinga Man Again."

> *Ngoa-ekele ana yi small resse dem don turn place for make chomeurs.*
> *Diplome dem don change statut*
> *Licencies na taximan, oda wan na benskinneurs.*
> *BTS na secretaries fo conna road.*
> *Some dem na bayam sellam.*
> *Les bacheliers na pharmaciens fo gazon.*
> *G.C.E O'Level, na cotinbanga weti cotiroler.*
> *Oda wan di work na fo banana farm.*
> *Brevete na chargeurs.*
> *Oda wan no cokseurs.*
> *G.C.E A'Level na broke stone,*
> *Some wan dem de dig sansan.*
> *CAP na quincaillers de la casse, certain des vendeurs de fruits.*
> *C.E.P.E na pousseurs,*
> *Some wan na chouk head.*
> *Some wan di voska na tapis.*
> *First School Leaving Certificate na aware,*
> *Oda wan na colonel major fo gardiannage.*
> *Pipi leke wi so we wi go fo finale,*
> *Man weh i fit nak ndamba,*
> *Man weh I fit slap ndenge,*
> *Man weh I get heart I fit go sell kemika fo Dubai.*
> *Yes Mbombo, all we na haut cadres,*
> *Categorie A fo ministere des sauveteurs.*

Wu sai wi own fruit de la croissance de no?
Na wi dis today, contri don fall so te na wi dis today
Double champion du monde de choko.

Ngoa-ekele and her younger sisters have become factories for moulding the unemployed.
Certificates have lost their intrinsic value.
Holders of the first degree have been reduced to driving taxis,
 while others carry passengers on motorcycles.
Holders of the BTS have become public letter writers,
 while others have become street hawkers.
Holders of pre-university diplomas are vendors of patent medicine.
Holders of the G.C.E. O'Level have become harvesters of palm fruits,
 while others tap rubber.
Holders of the B.E.P.C are motor park touts,
 others are hustlers.
Holders of the G.C.E Advanced Level crush stones,
 Others dig sand.
Holders of C.A.P peddle hardware,
 others are fruit vendors.
Holders of the C.E.P.E have become truck pushers,
others are porters,
 while others are carpet cleaners.
Holders of the First school Leaving Certificates are rank and file policemen,
 while others are security guards.
People like us who never had the opportunity to go to school
 Are forced to slave and sweat.
We can either play football or play music.
The brave ones can venture to go and sell chemicals in Dubai.
Yes, my friends, we are all Category A senior civil servants
 in the ministry of the unemployed.
Where, then, is our own share of the economic growth?
Here we are today, in a ruined economy and classified Among the Heavily Indebted Poor Countries.

Two things are obvious here. The first is that the kind of education delivered in Cameroon is obsolete. The second is that the system has little regard for meritocracy, and, as a result, tends to favour loyal mediocrity to critical excellence. Thus, if the situation has to improve, the educational system must continually adapt to the ever-changing needs of the global market place. In other words, just as the business world is adjusting its views to a changing society, so too the educational system must do the same. Benji Mateke also dwells on the same theme in "Boulot c'est Boulot" (2006).

> *Debout, Debout, debout, debout*
> *Tous les chomeurs chantent avec le sorcier Bantou, Benji Mateke.*
>
> *Donnez-moi aussi du boulot eh eh*
> *Moi aussi je veux travailler.*
> *Trouvez-moi un peu du boulot eh eh*
> *Moi aussi je veux travailler.*
>
> *Papaa m'a paye les etudes, j'ai eu mes diplomes,*
> *J'ai meme fait des formations, mais je n'ai pas du boulot oh*
> *Ah mama ah, je suis toujours au chomage.*
> *President Bamba ah, papa m'a paye les etudes, j'ai eu mes diplomes,*
> *J'ai meme fait des formations, mais je n'ai pas du boulot, President Esaka.*
>
> *Donnez-moi aussi du boulot eh eh,*
> *Ah mama ah, moi aussi je veux travailler.*
> *Rien que du boulot eh eh*
> *Trouvez-moi un peu du boulot eh eh,*
> *Moi aussi je veux travailler*
> *Ah mama ah oh.*
>
> *Wandji Claudine Koujou, toujours au service de l'humanite, la maman des Artistes.*
> *J'ai fait des milliers de demandes pour chercher du boulot*
> *Il y a toujours des redez-vous, mais jamais du travail,*
> *Quand j'etais a l'ecole, je voulais devenir medecin*

Si ce n'est pas medecin, je voulais devenir docteur.
Aujourd'hui j'ai eu tous mes diplomes, il n'ya toujours pas du boulot oh oh.
C'est encore papa qui me donne l'argent du loyer eh
C'est toujous mama qui depanne l'argent de poche eh eh.

Donnez-moi aussi du boulot eh eh
Moi aussi je veux travailler.
Moi je veux travailler eh eh
Trouvez-moi aussi du boulot eh eh
Moi aussi je veux travailler.

L'ecole en Afrique n'a plus de valeur.
L'ecole au Cameroun n'a plus sa valeur eh eh mama ah
Meme si tu es diplome, tu ne va pas travailler
Et meme si tu es qualifie, tu sera toujours au chomage.
J'ai perdu tout espoir oh Benji oh oh
Donnez-moi n'importe quoi, pourvu que je travaille
Oh mama oh, pour que je ne meurs pas de faim.

C'est moi le directeur general de la societe camerounaise de chomage, chomecam.
J'ai déjà recruite cinq million de jeunes de Mbanga
Et je recruit 24/24.
Les futures chomeurs de l'université de Soa, de Ngaoundere, de Buea,
De Dschang, de Douala et de Yaounde 1, je vous attends.
A chomecam, il n'y a pas de frais de dossier eh.

Boulot c'est boulot,
Il n'y a pas de choix eh eh
Boulot c'est boulot eh
Boulot c'est boulot eh
Boulot c'est boulot eh.

Si tu peux laver les voitures eh eh
C'est ca le boulot
Si tu peut faire ton bendskin eh
C'est ca le boulot.
Si tu peux vendre tes fruits a Njombe eh

C'est ca le boulot.
Boulot c'est boulot
Il n'y a plus le choix.

Taximen oh, on va faire comment?
We know know oh.
Comme ca
Chargeurs et laveur, how wi go do oh?
Comme ci.
Sauveteurs oh, vous allez casser les prix?
Jamais, jamais, on dit jamais.
On va alors faire comment eh?
Aristide Priso, l'homme du future l'argent n'a pas de couleur, Money no get colour.
Mbanga people, on va faire comment?
Bamenda people, wi go do how oh?
Souza people, on va faire comment?
Wolowoss oh, on fait gratis?
Jamais, jamais.
Boulot c'est boulot oh
Il n'y a plus de choix.

Stand up, stand up, stand up stand up.
All the unemployed, sing with the Bantu sorcerer, Benji Mateke.
Give me a job also eh eh.
I also want to work.
Find something useful for me to do eh eh.
I also want to work.

My father paid for my schooling, I obtained my diplomas
I also underwent professional training
But I don't have a job oh
Ah mama ah, I am still unemployed.
President Bamba ah, my father paid for my schooling,
And I obtained my diplomas.
I even underwent professional training
But I don't have a job President Esaka.

Give me a job eh eh
Ah mama ah, I also want to work

Nothing but a job eh eh
Find something useful for me to do
I also want to work
Ah mama ah ah.

Wandji Claudine Koujou, always at the service of humanity,
The matron of artists.
I have written thousands of applications for employment,
There have always been rendez-vous, but never a job.
When I was at school, I wanted to be a medical practitioner,
If not a medical practitioner, I would have loved to hold a Ph.D.
Today, I have all my degrees, but there is nothing for me to do.
My father still pays my house rents eh
It is always my mother who gives me pocket money.

Give me a job also eh eh.
I also want to work
I want to work eh eh
Find something useful for me to do
I also want to work.
Schools in Africa no longer have value.
Schools in Cameroon have lost their value eh eh mama ah.
Even if you are a graduate you cannot find employment.
And even if you are qualified, you will always remain unemployed.
I have lost all hope oh Benji oh oh.
Give me whatever is available provided I have work.
Oh mama oh, so that I should not die of hunger.

I am the General Manager of the Cameroon company of the unemployed, Chomecam.
I have already recruited five million youths at Mbanga
And I recruit 24/24.
The future unemployed of the universities of Soa, Ngaoundere, Buea,

> *Dschang, Douala and Yaounde 1, I am anxiously waiting for you.*
> *At Chomecam, there are no charges for applying oh.*
> *Work is work*
> *There is no choice eh eh*
> *Work is work*
> *Work is work*
> *Work is work.*
>
> *If you can wash cars eh eh*
> *It is work.*
> *If you can carry passengers on a motor cycle, It is work.*
> *If you can sell fruits at Njombe eh, it is work.*
> *Work is work,*
> *There is no longer a choice.*
>
> *Taxi drivers oh, what shall we do?*
> *We don't know.*
> *Like that.*
> *Truck loaders and car wash boys, what shall we do?*
> *Like this.*
> *Hawkers will you slash prices?*
> *No, No, they say No!*
> *What then shall we do eh?*
> *Aristide Priso, man of the future, money has no colour,*
> *Money has no colour.*
> *People of Mbanga, what shall we do?*
> *People of Bamenda, what shall we do?*
> *People of Souza, what shall we do?*
> *Prostitutes oh, shall we do it for free?*
> *No, No!*
>
> *Work is work*
> *There is no longer a choice.*

The scenario painted by Mateke in "Boulot c'est Boulot" (2006), is bleak, dismal and pathetic. Under normal circumstances, parents educate their children in order to make them independent and self-sufficient. The children on their part work hard to graduate in order to be able to fend for themselves and also to derive job satisfaction. That is why the protagonist in the song can say with confidence that:

> *When I was at school, I wanted to be a medical practitioner,*
> *If not a medical practitioner, I would have loved to hold a Ph.D.*

The implication here is that the protagonist nursed dreams of climbing up the educational and professional ladder. He is ready to work hard to achieve his objectives but, in today's Cameroon his dream is short lived because after graduating he could not find a suitable employment. The protagonist is further worried by the fact that in spite of his qualifications, he is still dependent on his parents for the necessities of life:

> *My father still pays my house rents,*
> *It is always my mother who gives me pocket money.*

The youth finds this state of affairs not only humiliating but unacceptable. However, the worst is yet to come. After waiting for a long time for an employment that is not forth-coming, the young man lost hope and, in desperation, is ready to accept anything provided it keeps him occupied:

> *Even if you are a graduate, you cannot work.*
> *And even if you are qualified, you will always remain unemployed.*
> *I have lost all hope oh Benji oh oh.*
> *Give me whatever is available provided I work.*
> *Oh mama oh, so that I should not die of hunger.*

The above is a cry of desperation degenerating into despair. It is a clear indication that the future for Cameroonian youths is, to say the least, gloomy.

Mateke, like Lapiro sees the informal sector as the only alternative open to the unemployed youths. But, the question that begs for an answer here is, does one need to go to school, obtain a university degree only to end up as a street vendor, a telephone booth operator or a seller of second hand clothing? However, unlike Lapiro who is optimistic about the future and who encourages the disillusioned youths not to surrender, Mateke is pessimistic and morose. Nevertheless, even Lapiro is sometimes so overwhelmed by the predicament of the youths and the downward turn which the whole country is taking that he decides to consign all those who are responsible for the quagmire to the maximum security prison in Yaounde in the song, "Tout le Monde a Kondengui":

> *Envoyez tout le monde a Kondengui!*
> *Tout le monde a Kondengui!*
> *Big Katika a Kondengui!*
> *Tout le ministres a Kondengui!*
> *Biensur! Biensur, Biensur!*
> *Je jure que yi own mandate dong shot...*
> *Dat be say njaka for njaka for we njaka*
> *Dem go come boulot for pay dang doh...*
> *Big Katika for Ngola and yi Nchinda dem say...*
> *Comme vous pouvez le constater,*
> *Cameroon dong capside...*
> *Yes mbombo, dis contri no well...*
>
> *Send everybody to Kondengui!*
> *Everybody to Kondengui!*
> *Big Katika to Kondengui!*
> *All his ministers to Kondengui!*
> *Sure! Sure! Sure!*
> *His own mandate has ended, take it from me, this implies that our great grand children*
> *Shall work to pay back these loans.*
> *Big Katika in Ngola and his lieutenants say...*
> *As you can see for yourselves, This country is topsy-turvy,*
> *Yes, my friend, this country is sick...*

The above outburst from Lapiro notwithstanding, the fact remains that Cameroonian protest musicians with Lapiro in the forefront, are largely optimistic about the future direction of Cameroon. They are aware that their music may not spark off an immediate revolution. But they are nevertheless convinced that it would at least conscientize an otherwise dormant people.

It is indeed a matter for regret that more African orature is studied in Western than in our own universities. Another problem is the refusal by our university authorities to accord sufficient attention to our traditional artists in spite of the fact that they demonstrate great mastery of the techniques of narrative or poetic composition. The flimsy excuse advanced is that the artists are largely illiterate in the Western sense of the word. But, the traditional artist does not need to hold a PhD or other lofty academic diplomas to be recognized. In fact, we find among our unsung storytellers, poets, and musicians highy ingenious and admirably creative artists like Lapiro de Mbanga who deftly weaves the art of words and create a special lingo of their own known as Lapiroism without holding a university degree.

Clearly, no educated Cameroonian writer has so far shown such a remarkable technical virtuosity and dexterity in the creation of a composite language. Thus, it is high time that we dispose of such misconceptions including that which questions the very existence of oral literature. It is high time for us to decolonize our educational system. We need to let our culture form the core of our curriculum. We need to let those indigenous artists who have a good mastery of our history, philosophy, and culture to teach our people. The over-riding question therefore is; how can our policy makers supplement the obvious deficiencies in the present education system in Cameroon? The answer lies in maintaining an organic continuity with our past. Patrick Mbunwe Samba in (Ongoun and Tcheho, 1985: 91) upholds this view when he postulates that

> *As a matter of fact, oral literature should become an all-important subject in all our educational institutions at all levels ... We should be proud to place our oral tradition in the school system rather than put subjects that have no bearing on our society just because such courses are done in metropolitan institutions. We should think more of what is relevant to us as a people, rather than copy wholesale and forcibly superimpose other people's value systems on our own, perhaps because our appetites were whetted by the colonial glamour.*

Therefore, what we need in Cameroon today is a new and genuine education system based on the fundamental principle which is the wellspring of our traditional system of education. That is, we need to implement the problem-posing concept of education. That is why I wholeheartedly endorse the view advanced by Ojoade in (Ongoum and Tcheho, 101) that "the quality of instruction at all levels has to be oriented towards inculcating the following values : moral and spiritual values in inter-personal and human relations". And that this instruction must be geared towards "self-realization, better human relationships, the right type of values and attitudes for the survival of the individual and the Cameroonian society." This return to a full understanding of traditional principles and an understanding of how they can work especially in changing times and circumstances is what Cameroonians really need if they are to break away from the cultural limbo that is destroying the social health of their society.

I agree that this is easier said than done especially because government efforts have been diverted to the services of capitalism, militarism and allied interests. The deepening economic recession and the international financial crunch are also forcing Cameroonians, like their counterparts elsewhere, to take advantage of the conspicuous absence of a unified cultural ethos in their society to indulge their instincts. Hence, it is common to find a growing number of Cameroonians struggling to get all the advantages out of life without attempting to give anything back to society in return. In fact, a few years ago, Cameroon was rated by Transparency International as the most corrupt country in the world.

The point must however be made that in spite of the ethical deficiencies in the present educational system, it does have several advantages. For example, it provides the secular, pluralistic and market values necessary for the functioning of the political and economic institutions of the country. Consequently, all is not yet lost as the system can be revamped following the road map proposed by Dasylva in (Kaschula, 2001: 187):

> *The teaching of culture and traditional values must begin from nursery education. School curriculum right from the nursery school must be designed to reflect the significance of the nation's cultural values and oral tradition, and as a matter of national policy. Similarly, a re-orientation of oral literary scholarship must be considered in the universities for the purpose of accommodating practical learning of oral*

> *performances in poetry, storytelling, songs, chants, etc. It is a sure way of ensuring continuity.*

The need to begin the teaching of orature from the nursery school has been underscored by A.F. Ogunsola in (E. Mokwunye, 1978: V):

> *It is in the lower primary classes that the very foundation of all our education is laid. A solid foundation to education cannot be laid outside a child's culture. It is therefore important that we get the child to understand and appreciate the gifts of his society in a planned and systematic way. A child is, of course, born into a culture and not born with it.*

Orature can therefore help children especially in contemporary society to grapple with the psychological and moral problems of growing up.

My main intention in this book as I have explained in the Introduction, is to draw attention to the richness of the indigenous knowledge contained in Cameroon orature, and to demonstrate how this knowledge can be used to resolve the post-colonial problems of governance in contemporary Cameroon. I also explained that in this chapter, I intend to highlight the educational potential of the orature and to encourage its vigorous promotion in our school system. The goal is to demonstrate how the ethical and moral gap in the existing education system can be filled by the moral precepts embedded in the orature. It is not my intention however to idealize orature, neither do I pretend that orature alone can be used in our educational system. Rather, my objective is to address the complementary relation that should exist between orature and what is being taught in our schools. That is why I am making a strong case for orature to be included in the curriculum at all levels. That, in my opinion, will help to transform the existing concept of education from the "banking" to the "problem-posing". This transformation is all the more necessary because as Freire (1982), has demonstrated,

> *Problem-posing education is revolutionary futurity. Hence it is prophetic (and, as such, hopeful). Hence, it affirms men as beings who transcend themselves, who move forward and look ahead, for whom immobility*

> *represents a fatal threat, for whom looking at the past must only be a means of understanding more clearly what and who they are so that they can more wisely build the future.*

Since orature is used to educate the young and also to remind the adults of their responsibilities, I will use two oral tales to illustrate how orature can be used to prepare our youth for responsible adult life and ultimately contribute to healthy social development. I will also use some proverbs to emphasize the necessity of reminding the elders of their social and moral obligation – that of living by precepts.

    The first tale is titled "The Feast in the Sky" or "Why the Tortoise has cracks on its shell". Animals play a prominent role in the oral tale because Cameroonians live in close proximity to the animals that share their land. In many of the tales, the people attribute human feelings and desires to particular animals; and even derive ethical ideals from their behavior. This is evident in the trickster tale.

    Trickster characters differ from society to society and assume different roles for their respective audiences. In the Grassfields of Bamenda for example, the animal trickster is invariably the flamboyant spider while in the Forest zone around Widikum it is the ubiquitous tortoise. No matter what names they assume, these wily, smallish trickster figures tend to have several things in common. They are usually small and weak, but they are also shrewd, cunning, greedy, exhibitionistic, and unpredictable. Consequently, they are the best instruments for commenting on the opposition between wit and force. Their main preoccupation seems to be to make up for their physical and other disabilities with a very high degree of intelligence which they often misuse either to deceive or cheat. The fact that they almost always emerge victorious in their exploits does not mean that the people approve of their practice of gratuitous roguery. Rather, the people see in the trickster figures a reflection of the vices they condemn, the follies they ridicule, and the evils with which they must contend. The classic tale in which the tortoise uses his cool independence and agreeable nature to dupe the birds and disrupt social equilibrium is often told to illustrate tortoise's crafty underhanded ingenuity.

The Feast in the Sky
Once upon a time, there was famine on earth because of lack of rain. As a result, there was nothing for Tortoise to eat and he was dying of hunger. One day, he overheard the birds discussing about a feast in the sky. He approached them and politely begged to accompany them to the feast. The birds agreed very reluctantly because they knew Tortoise well. But he managed to convince them that he would be of good behavior. So, they lent him a feather each to enable him to fly with them to the feast.

On their way to the party, he convinced the birds that they should take a name each. He went on to tell them that his own name was "All of You". The unsuspecting birds agreed and they continued their journey to the sky.

They were well received at the party. Tortoise was highly impressed by the sumptuous dishes placed on the table that he immediately devised a means to outwit his companions. As soon as they were invited to the table, he asked the birds if they remembered the name he took on the way. They naively chirped in unison, "All of You". He then asked their gullible hosts, for whom the food was served. The unsuspecting hosts replied, for "All of You". Tortoise then reminded the birds that since that was the name he adopted, it meant that the food was for him alone. He advised them to be patient and wait for their own share. So he sat down and greedily consumed all the food while the birds watched in silent anger. When he finished eating and nothing was forthcoming for them, the hungry and angry birds decided there and then to make Tortoise pay for his mischief. They took back their feathers and flew to earth leaving Tortoise stranded in the sky.

Perplexed, Tortoise begged the last bird that when he reached earth, he should tell his wife to bring out all the mattresses and pillows and lay them in such a way that he could land on them safely. The bird agreed. But, on reaching earth, he told Tortoise's wife to spread out all the available hardware.

Meanwhile, Tortoise was watching from the sky. When he saw that his wife had spread out what he thought were mattresses and pillows, he jumped from the sky and landed heavily on the hardware thereby cracking his shell – an event which explains the Tortoise's appearance today.

In this tale, Tortoise and the birds live in a traditional society. The ideological matrix holding the society together is collective responsibility, the responsibility of the group for the well-being of the members. It is this community oriented thinking which prompts the birds to try to save Tortoise from the effects of the famine. Of course the Birds know Tortoise for what he is, an ingenious trickster. They also know that underlying his suave appearance is a calculating ruthlessness. But, since their culture makes room for temperament especially when it does not threaten the stability of the established order, they try to accommodate social misfits like the Tortoise. But, Tortoise who is the equivalent of the perfect courtier of times gone by who gets his way through seduction, deception, and subtle strategy, is not guided by the interest of the group. Rather, he is an extremely individualistic and ethically non-conforming character. That explains why he appears as a single and often isolated character.

The taking of the name "All of You" by Tortoise is an act of self–promotion. By allowing him to take that name, the birds unwittingly transfer power to him thereby making him their leader. Tortoise, on his part, is quick to accept the power, but refuses to recognize the responsibility that goes with it. As a result, he feels that he can ignore the birds from whom he derives his power. He however forgets that in social relationships, everything, which disrupts the orderly life of the group, must be removed. That is why when his code of behavior which is based on unmitigated egotism poses a threat to the well-being of the birds, they decide to punish him by dissociating themselves from him.

The Tortoise symbolizes man in his most primitive and animal state. It gives the impression that man is congenitally wicked and evil. There is no doubt that man's environment is hostile and therefore requires great intelligence and ingenuity for survival. But it is precisely in this struggle for survival that man exposes his negative traits. In the tale under discussion, the Tortoise is faced with the natural feeling of hunger which might eventually lead to starvation. Therefore, he uses every means at this disposal to procure food for himself in order to assuage his hunger. In trying to satisfy his desires however, he over-reaches himself and crashes. The bitter truth here is clear. The negative qualities portrayed by the Tortoise are not only prevalent in the Cameroonian society today but are caused by the same instincts of survival and self-preservation that have led the Tortoise to over-reach himself. Cameroonians, like their counterparts elsewhere want to live in opulence and ostentation. They want to send their children to prestigious schools. They want to own landed property, vast mansions, flashy cars, and well-furnished bank accounts. In order to achieve their goals, they are ready to cheat, defraud, and steal. In short to seek maximum rewards with minimum efforts. But, in trying to satisfy their greed, they abuse the rights and privileges that have been entrusted to them. They undermine the rights of fellow Cameroonians and, above all, threaten the stability of the country. The point must however be made that the traditional Cameroonian society which produced such trickster tales were not against the inordinate acquisition of wealth. In fact, they were basically materialistic. But, as Achebe in (Okoh, 240) points out,

> *A man's position in society was usually determined by his wealth. All the four titles in my village were taken not given, and each one had its price. But in those days wealth meant the strength of your arm. No one became rich by swindling the community or stealing government money. In fact, a man who was guilty of theft immediately lost all his titles. Today, we have kept the materialism and thrown away the spirituality which should keep it in check.*

The story of the Tortoise therefore raises one important question, namely: How do we pursue our goals and achieve our objectives in life? The answer surely is not by following the covetousness, wanton greed, and gross immorality of the outrageous Tortoise. Rather it lies in the right values like dignity, humaneness, and other positive vaues contained in our orature. The story also calls on us to discard the Machiavellan adage that the end justifies the means and to replace it with the traditional wisdom that the means of achieving our goals are as important as the goals themselves.

The second tale, "The Poor Hunter", is about the corrupting power of privilege, position and success.

The Poor Hunter
There lived a man who was very poor. He had lost his parents and poverty was his only friend in this world. He took to hunting but the animals seemed to avoid him. He spent days in the forest but returned home without shooting even a bird. One day, he decided to go deep into the forest in the hope of finding a good catch. After walking for a long distance and finding nothing, he decided to rest under a tree. Since he was hungry and had no food, his eyes searched the trees in the hope of seeing a ripe fruit. Instead, he saw an old woman sitting not far from him. He was stricken by fear but somehow managed to find the courage to greet her. She asked him what he was doing alone in the forest. He narrated his sad story to her and she took pity on him. She asked him to stand up and turn round with his back toward her. He obeyed. She then asked him to strip naked. He reluctantly did and suddenly found himself in a big town.

The townspeople welcomed him as if they had been expecting him. They immediately took him to the palace, clothed him in royal robes and crowned him their chief. The man was overjoyed to find himself the object of such attention. He was then conducted round the palace. When they came to a particular door, the palace guide stopped and said to the new chief. "My Lord, everything that I have shown you are under your command. But, you must never open this door. It is a sacred door."

For several years the chief ruled or rather led his people happily. He listened to their complaints and solved their problems. In short, he did everything in his power to promote the collective aspirations of his people for stability and peace. But, with time, the chief became dissatisfied with the fact that the power which he wielded was fettered. He wondered why a successful chief like himself should be prohibited from opening a mere door. But, he failed to understand that by questioning the nature of the power and authority which he held, he was inevitably aiming at absolute power.

During the end of year ceremonies which were conducted to mark the end of a successful harvest season. The chief threw a huge feast for his people. After the last guest had left, the visibly happy chief retired to his private quarters. On his way, he passed in front of the "sacred door". Suddenly, the caution which he had exercised all along was swept away by the afterglow of power drunkenness. He moved to the door and opened it. He stepped inside and closed the door behind him. He found himself standing naked in front of the old woman sitting under the iroko tree. "Here are your things" she said, handing him his rags, spear and cutlass.

When the hunter meets with his good luck in the form of the ubiquitous old woman, he is happy but, at the same time, he is careful not to allow his good luck to enter his head. Thus, rather than allow his dancing feet to impel him forward, he steps back and takes a careful look at where he is going. This cautious act accounts for his successful reign. But, in the heat of success, especially after the feast, he becomes emotional and feels invulnerable. That is when he over-reaches himself and opens the "sacred door". Hence, his good luck becomes more dangerous than his original bad luck. As a poor man, he contented himself with the little he had. But, when he becomes a successful chief, his good luck deludes him into thinking that his good fortune will carry him through. In so doing, he forgets that "there is nothing more intoxicating than success and nothing more dangerous" The ultimate lesson of this tale is therefore," the greater the power, the more dangerous the abuse."

The first tale, "The Feast in the Sky", is told to reinforce group solidarity. It encourages the people to develop a strong sense of belonging. It also helps to strengthen the collective conscience or moral integration among members of a community. The second tale, "The Poor Hunter", warns against vaulting ambition. Both tales deal with greed and its deleterious consequences. They also comment on the condition of man and the state of his society. Finally, they suggest ways of improving the society. So far, I have concentrated on the oral tale, but other forms of orature like proverbs and the popular or protest songs also tell us much about our past and how we can use it today to prepare for tomorrow.

If the oral tale is mainly used in the education of the young, the proverb is used for the education of both the young and the old. That is why it serves as a favourite vehicle for society-sanctioned instruction. Generally, every situation has a corresponding proverb although a proverb may not necessarily apply only to one particular situation. Since proverbs have many functions, the ones I have selected for use here are those which are often used to remind adults of their responsibilities especially towards the youth. Of course, there are proverbial expectations of the young in their relationship with adults but that is not my immediate concern.

My contention here is that if we are to examine a repertoire of Cameroonian proverbs dealing with the responsibilities of elders in the community, we are likely to notice striking discrepancies between proverbial prescriptions of behavior and the realities in contemporary Cameroon. That is, elders who in traditional society were ultimately responsible for the formulation of the proverbs that govern life in the community are, in contemporary contexts behaving in ways that are incongruous with their elderly status. For example, they are responsible for the pervasive corruption, gross mismanagement and the perpetuation of the country's economic afflictions; for the absolute lack of responsibility, restraint and tolerance that necessarily accompany good governance; for the drastic truncation of the freedom of criticism; and for collaborating with the neo-colonial powers. In short, they are responsible for the imbroglio in which Cameroon finds itself. It is obvious from the above that

Cameroonian elders have, for the most part, abdicated their moral responsibilities to their country in general and to the youth in particular.

The social organization of most Cameroonian societies it will be recalled is based on the philosophical assumption that age and the experience that goes with it are indispensable to the well-being of the community. Hence the proverbs: "a village without elders is like a well without water"; "when there are no elders in a town, the town is disorganized"; "an adult does not sit and watch while the she-goat suffers the pains of childbirth tied to a post"; and "the presence of an elder in the market place should ensure that no child's neck is crooked". These proverbs indicate that Cameroonians respect age because of the sagacity and the perspicacity that go with it. They also believe that longevity is the best schooling in life. That is why they expect their elders to be responsible for their actions and to act responsibly. These convictions are again encapsulated in the following proverbs: "good palm-wine becomes better with age to a good drinker; "a new broom sweeps clean, but the old broom knows better all the corners of the house"; "the youth may have as many clothes as the elder but he will not have as many rags"; "kola is ripe only in the mouth of an elder"; and "what an old man can see sitting down, a child cannot see standing up".

The implication of these proverbs is that elders are respected mainly because of their maturity and wealth of experience. That is why no matter their social status, elders are seen as the custodians of tradition and are given the respect due to them. N.A. Fadipe in (Ongoum and Tchehu, 405), stresses the importance attached to this principle of seniority in Yoruba life. According to him, it operates

> *To the disregard of wealth, rank or sex and those who flout it do so at the risk of serious communal disapproval. In keeping with the principle, elders have the last word in arguments with the young; they can count on the youth to defer to them and render them service, including coming to their defence and assistance in confrontations in which age might place them at a disadvantage.*

What Fadipe says about the Yoruba also applies to Cameroonians. But the prestige and privileges which the elders enjoy by virtue of their age, also impose certain obligations on them. For instance, they are expected to set the right examples for the youth to follow by always acting with propriety and behaving with proper decorum. This is contained in the following proverb: "the lead horse sets the pace for those following". Fadipe substantiates this point when he said in (Ongoum and Tcheho, 406) that

> In order to earn the respect due to his superior years, a man must demonstrate some wisdom and experience. He must be prepared to discharge the responsibilities and duties of this position, and must show himself to be morally worthy of the respect paid to him.

I will illustrate Fadipe's assertion with an incident that took place not long ago in the village of Bamenda-Nkwe in the North West Region of Cameroon. A child accompanied his father to a funeral. As is usually the case, the child carried both the chair and the raffia bag of his father. In the course of the funeral ceremony, the elders were served food. The father ate everything and forgot about the child who accompanied him. The youngster, who watched his father's act of thoughtlessness with disdain, abandoned his father at the funeral and returned home. Another elder who watched the incident, chuckled and cited the following proverb, "the elder who eats all his food without leaving some for the child will carry his own chair home". The point being made here is that the relationship between the old and the young is based on reciprocity. Youth will defer to age if the latter behaves responsibly. But, when an elder chooses to behave in any way that does not befit his elderly status, he should expect disrespect from the youth. This principle of reciprocal responsibility is metaphorically rendered by the proverb "the hand of the child cannot reach the high shelf, nor can that of an older person pass through the neck of a calabash". For a child to attain his objective, he may need the help of an elder. On the other hand, there are tasks which the elder can perform only with the help of a child. As Ojinmah (67) puts it,

> *In the traditional society, the people themselves have a say in what happens and how their lives are to be governed. Morality is held in high regard and the actions of individuals and the society are motivated by what they feel is in the interest of the community. The traditional mores and beliefs foster the social and moral ethics ensuring mutual co-existence of all ... But most importantly, the system of government is intrinsically interwoven with these mores.*

As a result of the rapid socio-economic, political and cultural change which Cameroon has undergone and is still undergoing, various forms of vice crept into the society and weakened the unified cultural ethos. Consequently, Cameroonians, especially the older generation, began to be alienated from the traditional ways and values and to develop a code of behavior based on crass individualism. This confusion of values might have prompted the elders to abdicate their traditional responsibilities to society in general and the youth in particular. The youth, in turn, are quick to retaliate by repudiating their obligations to society and to the elderly. This, to my mind, is at the root of the moral decadence and socio-political tensions that characterize contemporary life in Cameroon. Thus, it is common today to find Cameroonian youth indulging in such deviant behaviors as heavy drinking and smoking, reckless driving, indecent dressing, sexual promiscuity, cyber criminality popularly known as scamming, and downright rebellion against authority and authority figures.

It is obvious from the above that the youth of Cameroon are very angry with their elders especially those in positions of authority for not being models of rectitude, for marginalizing them and for refusing to use their knowledge and abilities. As the Okedijis in (Ongoum and Tcheho, 412) put it,

> *When, with the introduction of a foreign culture, problems become more complicated, varied and differentiated... it is the young people who are brought into immediate experience of the changed conditions. Hence a regime in which youth has no chance of making its wishes known is not likely to be best adjusted to meet situations as they present themselves from day to day, and, consequently, is not likely to make progress.*

Cameroonian youth are painfully aware of this fact. That is why they are shocking their elders with calculated acts of rebellion. Therefore, if the elders who now control virtually everything in the country want Cameroon to make any meaningful progress on the path towards economic growth and modernization, they must appease the youth by incorporating them into decision making bodies and by creating enough room for their inputs especially in the resolution of important social, political and economic issues. In doing so they should bear in mind the proverb that says "when a sheep is old, it is suckled by the young ones". Furthermore, if they, as elders, want to continue to influence Cameroon's perception and sense of direction, they should go back to the ways of their fathers and re-assume the social and ethical responsibilities which they have shamelessly discarded. That is, they should live by precepts. They should also bear in mind that "the child of a snake is also a snake". That is, a child takes after its parents especially their negative traits.

Here are some additional proverbs culled from the everyday experience of the people. They are used to teach the importance of togetherness and group solidarity; to inculcate the necessity for mutual respect, tolerance, and moderation; to reiterate the need for appropriate action; to ensure compliance with religious norms; to remind the people of the necessity of circumspection, and the importance of recognizing one's limitations. It should be borne in mind that Cameroonian proverbs are similar to proverbs elsewhere and that the fundamental values reflected in the proverbs are, for the most part, universal.

> *A fly without an adviser usually follows the corpse into the grave.*
> *A river that travels alone often meanders.*
> *The dog that would get lost would not listen to the whistle of the hunter.*
> *The man who brings ant-ridden faggots into his hut should not grumble when lizards begin to pay him visits.*
> *If a witch enters the house, it is because somebody left the door open.*

He who chooses to live by the roadside should not be tired of greetings from passersby.
A person who has not secured a place on the floor should not begin to look for a mat.
A traveler to distant places should not make enemies.
We do not bypass a man and enter his house.
We do not apply an ear-pick to an eye.
Ashes fly back in the face of the thrower.
Bending down to a dwarf does not prevent you from rising to your full height afterwards.
Only a foolish man can go after a tiger with bare hands.
When you dig a hole of wickedness, make it shallow for you may be the one to fall into it.
He who despises another despises himself.
He who swallows a pestle will have to sleep standing.
The sun will shine on those who stand before it shines on those who kneel under it.
A man who swallows a bush mango seed should know the size of his anus.
The fly that struts around on a mound of excrement wastes his time; the mound will always be greater than the fly.
Unity among the cattle makes the lion lie down hungry.
Anybody who reaps where he did not sow may one day sow where he will not reap.
A short man hangs his bag where he can reach it.
However hard he may try, the tortoise cannot stretch himself beyond the confines of his shell.
If you look in one direction for too long, your neck will become stiff.
The inquisitive eye will only blind its own sight.
One who talks too much has very little time to do other things.
Lying will marry you a wife but will not keep her.
A cat keeps its claws hidden until it meets a mouse.
You cannot welcome a leper and shun his handshake.
Whenever godfatherism and palm greasing are preferred to scholarship, creativity, efficiency and experience, mediocrity reigns supreme.
If a fish wants to rot it begins from the head.
No matter how much one can lie, one cannot lie to himself.

> *No matter how far you walk along the path of a river, you cannot claim to have crossed it.*
> *Do not speak of the high cost of milk in the presence of a Fulani man.*
> *When a man of cunning dies, a man of cunning buries him.*
> *He who sells sand as salt will receive stones as money.*
> *A crocodile may live in the river but it will never be a fish.*
> *To be a good liar, you must have a good memory.*
> *If you set a trap of lies, it catches a game of lengthy explanations.*
> *Do not conclude that nobody is seeing you just because you do not see anybody looking at you.*
> *Only a woman knows the father of her child.*
> *The mouth cannot claim to be ignorant of what is inside the stomach.*
> *A man of sense does not go on hunting bush rodents when his age mates are after big game.*
> *If you do not know your destination, any road will do.*
> *Follow the river and you will find the sea*

Therefore, what is imperative today is that Cameroonians both old and young must make a conscious effort to refamiliarize themselves with, and reassimilate their cultural values. For that to become a reality, our educational policy makers must follow the advice of Oyekan Owomoyela in (Ongoum and Tcheho, 414) and ensure that orature reassumes the educational role it played in the traditional context:

> *The goal of policy makers must therefore be to ensure that a thorough grounding in the ways of our fathers is a mandatory and significant part of the upbringing of youth, and this can be done by making folklore in all its ramifications a central part of the educational curriculum, and a mandatory subject for all. By so doing we might in time achieve, once again, societies in which the observance of proper form translates into stability, harmony, and collective ease. By so doing, we would be able to claim, as we cannot now, that our folklore accurately reflects the values we live by.*

CHAPTER THREE
POPULAR SONGS AND PERCEPTIONS OF NATIONHOOD

> *Nation building entails inventing a complex but dynamic social and political system through a social contract, with all its component parts that takes care of the whole of human nature in all its essence and substance. It should also seek to include all the sectional interests and meets the aspirations of all the individuals and constituent groups within the collectivity, or that' imagined community,' so as to attain the goal of political unity to become a self-regulating transformational totality, and yet be socially liberating, without depending solely on foreign elements (Piaget, 1970:97).*

I made the point earlier on that the nation called Cameroon today was created by European colonizers for their own interests. Thus, from the very beginning, there was no intention whatsoever of building Cameroon into a country with its own identity and free from foreign influences. At independence, these foreign powers chose their own local collaborators whom they imposed on the unsuspecting Cameroonians. Thus, post-independence Cameroonian leaders are, in effect, representatives of neo-colonial powers and agents of international institutions. Since they do not have the mandate of Cameroonians on whose behalf they claim to speak, it follows, logically, that they cannot be entrusted with the task of nation building. Hence, the urgent political problem still facing Cameroonians today is the crisis of nationhood. That explains why the selected defiant artists have not only refused to be at the beck and call of Cameroonian politicians, but have used their music to fulminate against the unpatriotic politicians for their role in the socio-economic quagmire and widespread political malaise in the country orchestrated by bad governance. As Charles Nnolim (2000:2-3) has remarked,

> *In a society mainly vulgarized by a majority of the vulgar rich, of vulgar philistines with plebeian tastes and propensities, the society is not only endangered but traumatized. Culture looks beyond vulgar wealth, beyond the febrile pursuit of the false symbols of life, beyond the rude display of meretricious and garish symbols of affluence, beyond ill-bred foul-mouthed bragging about earthly possessions.*

The protest artists are fuuly aware of the above but, they do not despair. Rather, they are convinced that they can, through their protest songs, respond to the many grievances and demands from those to whom poverty and misery have become faithful companions, and also help to change the future course of society for the better. That is why they express their concerns on behalf of the suffering masses in the shared belief that what should be encouraged and promoted in Cameroon today is the overall interests of the public and not the narrow interests of some self-centred and bigoted political authority. That also explains why they have used the medium of their songs as "counter-power," to set some critical standards by which Cameroonians can assess their hitherto irrepressible leaders and also rebuild their country in their own image. Thus, the protest musicians have engaged in deconstructing and constructing the image and identity of postcolonial Cameroon.

I have selected four major intrepid protest musicians for detailed study in this chapter. They are, Lapiro de Mbanga, Longue Longue, Prince Yerima Afo Akom and Andre Marie Tala. But, where necessary, I have used excerpts from songs by other Cameroonian protest musicians to reinforce the point that I am making. It is worth noting that all the musicians whose songs are analysed in this chapter take sides with the common people whose lived experience of hunger, deprivation and uncertainty constitute the subject matter of the songs. In other words, the protest musicians use their songs to articulate the pressing socio-political and economic issues of the day and to awaken their society from the stupor into which it has unwittingly allowed itself to sink. This chapter therefore proffers the argument that the protest songs under study typify the responses of the downtrodden Cameroonians to their post-colonial conflicts and tensions. It also examines the crisis of nationhood fron the perspectives of the following sub-headings: cultural (mis) representation, the colonial policy of divide and rule, political corruption and the flagrant abuse of power, the pathological greed of the privileged and the mighty, exploitation and oppression of the masses, and power alternation in Cameroon.

Cultural (Mis)Representation of Nationhood

The term "cultural (mis) representation" or ethnocentrism is used here to refer to the deliberate denigration of indigenous Cameroonian cultures and the elevation of European cultures. It was one of the effective weapons used by the imperialists to subjugate the colonized. Nanda and Warms (1998:6) define ethnocentrism as,

> *The notion that one's culture is superior to any other. It is the idea that other cultures should be measured by the degree to which they live up to our cultural standards. We are ethnocentric when we view other cultures through the narrow lens of our own culture or social position.*

Ethnocentrism as a cultural phenomenon is common place in the sense that most people in the world tend to regard their own culture as superior. But, ethnocentrism takes on a negative condition and becomes destructive when it is used to shut others out and provide the basis for derogatory evaluations. As Edward Said (1980:78) has observed,

> *Imperialism was the theory, colonialism the practice of changing the uselessly unoccupied territories of the world into useful new versions of the European metropolitan society. Everything in those territories that suggested waste, disorder, unaccounted resources, was to be converted into productivity, order, taxable, potentially developed wealth. You get rid of most of the offending human and animal blight-whether because it simply sprawls untidily all over the place or because it roams around unproductively and unaccounted – and you confine the rest to reservations, compounds, native homelands, where you can count, tax, use them profitably, and you build a new society on the vacated*

space. Thus was Europe reconstructed abroad, its 'multiplication in space' successfully projected and managed. The result was a widely varied group of little Europes scattered throughout Asia, Africa, and the Americas, each reflecting the circumstances, the specific instrumentalities of the parent culture, its pioneers, its vanguard settlers. All of them were similar in one major respect – despite the differences, and that was that their life was carried with an air of normality.

That was exactly what the European colonial system of education set out to do. Schools in Cameroon were obliged to teach European history, geography, literature. They were also compelled to highlight the accomplishments of Europeans at the expense of Cameroonian heroes and traditional culture. European ethnocentrism not only exaggerated the differences between European and Cameroonian cultures, it also perceived Cameroonian cultures in terms of stereotypes. That is, it involved invidious comparisons which ennobled European cultures and degraded Cameroonian cultures. The Cameroonian popular musician, Donny Elwood in his successful album "Negro et Beau" (1997) is reacting against the restrictive and limiting orientation of extreme European ethnocentrism especially its rejection of Cameroonian cultures:

On dit qu'un negro n'est jamais beau
On dit qu'un negro est toujours un petit macro
Toujours un petit escro
Toujour un petit rigolot
Toujours un rigolot qui n'aime que le fafio.

They say that a negro is never handsome.
They say that a negro is always a small crook
Always a small swindler
Always a little jester
Always a jester who loves only money.

The implementation of this malignant policy of ethnocentrism started with the deliberate denigration of indigenous Cameroonian cultures. Europe was then projected as the centre of the world and European culture became the standard measuring rod for any other culture. In other words, European culture became universal and any other culture that did not conform to it was considered as marginal. That was the philosophy used to legitimize European imperialism. Achebe (1965:60) was reacting to the unexamined assumption that "universal" is synonymous with "European" when he said that:

> *I should like to see the word "universal" banned altogether until such a time as people cease to use it as synonyms for the narrow self-serving parochialisms of Europe until their horizon extends to include the entire world.*

Each colonial power had its own colonial policy. The British, for example, were interested in the indigenization of the occupied territory. That was why they adopted the policy of Indirect Rule which allowed them to use traditional rulers and elite to work on their behalf. The French, on their part, were more paternalistic and therefore practiced the policy of assimilation.

With colonialism firmly entrenched, the colonial masters embarked on the search for native auxiliaries of the colonial administration and for recruits into the new colonial army. It will be recalled that some of the pre-colonial societies which now make up post-colonial Cameroon were stateless while others were centralized. But the colonialists never bothered to take this important factor into consideration in their choice of the tribes they preferred to work with. As a result, some societies which, in the pre-colonial times had been basically stateless, were given precedence by the colonial administration over pre-colonial centralized societies. That explains how some pre-colonial stateless societies came to inherit the post-colonial state in Cameroon.

The colonial administration also hand-picked those to whom they arbitrarily gave the warrant to rule. Some of these were nonentities whose only qualification was their malleability. Others, who were hitherto considered as outcasts, had no compunction in oppressing the very society which had under the pre-colonial era looked upon and treated them with contempt. These people who were functioning as links between the colonial administration and the indigenous people – court messengers, interpreters, teachers, clerks and warrant chiefs were noted for their high-handedness and were consequently hated. Unfortunately, it is to these symbols of colonialism and oppression that political power was handed at independence.

As is to be expected, this new breed of black administrators and leaders approached their new responsibilities with the "chop-make-I-chop palaver finish" philosophy. In other words, they substituted the erstwhile colonial administration with a more insidious form of government which allowed them to wield almost absolute power over the country. Since this new government was rootless and also lacked legitimacy, it inevitably imposed more than one standard of behavior and more than one code of conduct on the people which were more often than not in conflict. The result was that misappropriation of national resources became almost a patriotic duty, and assiduity became an empty word. Lapiro de Mbanga expounds on this issue in "Qui ne'st rien n'a rien":

> *Which kanna kondri bi dis?*
> *You work leke jakass*
> *If you no de fo equipe national no man go tell you asiah.*
> *Which kanna kondri bi dis?*
> *Meme sep you get une opportunite*
> *If you no de fo pays organisateur dem go barre you sai by sai.*
> *Which kanna kondri bi dis?*
> *You lek you work leke how oh*
> *You lek you digam leke gron bif*
> *If you no de fo club fo toiteurs you own suffa no go finish.*
> *Na las heure be heure oh, Tara.*
>
> *What type of a country is this?*
> *Even if you work like a donkey*
> *If you don't belong to the circle of the privileged,*
> *Nobody will appreciate your efforts.*
> *What type of a country is this?*
> *Even if you have an opportunity,*
> *If you are not among those in power, they will block you at all ends.*
> *What type of a country is this?*
> *No matter how hard you work*

> *Even if you dig like a rat mole,*
> *If you are not in the club of swindlers,*
> *Your efforts will be in vain.*
> *It is the last hour which counts, my brother.*

Thus, the first thing that all the colonized and disempowered people must do after political independence is to reclaim and rehabilitate their old cultural tradition and its values. In other words, to go back to the "school of redress." Amilcar Cabral articulated (1973:42) this point as follows:

> *A people who free themselves from foreign domination will be free culturally only if, without complexes and without underestimating the importance of positive accretions from the oppressor and other cultures, they return to the upward path of their own culture, which is nourished by the living reality of its environment and which negates both harmful influences and any kind of subjection to foreign culture. Thus, it may be seen that if imperialist domination has the vital need to practice cultural oppression, national liberation is necessarily an act of culture.*

Achebe (1975:8) also called on his fellow Africans to rescue their past heritage from the colonial misrepresentation and biased stereotyping to which it has been subjected for so long. He sees this correction of the prejudices which generations of western detractors have created about the black man as the first step to any meaningful progress.

> *This is my answer to those who say that a writer should be writing about contemporary issues – about politics in 1964, about the last coup d'etat. Of course, these are all legitimate themes for a writer but as far as I am concerned, the fundamental theme must first be disposed of. This theme - put quite simply - is that African people did not hear of culture for the first time from Europeans, that their societies were not mindless but frequently had a philosophy of great depth and value and beauty, that they had poetry, and, above all, they had dignity. It is this dignity that many African people all but lost during the colonial period, and it is this that they must regain.*

Achebe is here making a case " for re-establishing contacts with familiar landmarks of yesteryear and then re-starting the journey of modernization under indigenous impetus". Mazrui (21) expressed similar views in the following passage:

> But when all is said and done, the most important cultural conflict occurring in Africa is between western civilization and indigenous forces. If instability in the continent is a symptom of cultures at war, perhaps Africa's identity may survive the ravages of westernization after all. It is still true to say that Africans in the twentieth century are becoming acculturated faster than were, for example, the Jews in the first millennium of their dispersal. But the war of cultures is by no means over in Africa. It is almost as if the indigenous ancestors have been aroused from the dead, and are fighting back to avert the demise of Africanity. In their immediate consequences decay and instability are a matter of lament. But in their longer term repercussions, they may be a matter for celebration.

Cameroonian protest musicians share the views of Achebe and Mazrui that instead of wallowing in self-pity, Cameroonians should rise up and situate themselves in history in order to give themselves the identity, pride and confidence which they need to reconstruct their present. This is essentially what Elwood is saying in the following lines:

> On dit qu'un negro n'est jamais beau
> Il y a des negro toujours beaux
> Chicago a Soweto
> Je suis negro et je suis beau.
>
> They say that negroes are congenitally ugly
> But there are negroes who are always handsome
> Chicago to Soweto
> I am a negro and I am handsome.

In the above song, Elwood refuses to carry the burden of defeat and inferiority complex imposed on him by the imperialists. That is why he passionately declares his pride in being black and beautiful. This is the kind of a re-awakened self-confidence and a sense of self-worth which the musicians want their people to regain in order to develop a sense of pride in their traditional life and culture.

The Colonial Policy of Divide and Rule

When the African continent was arbitrarily partitioned after the infamous Berlin Conference of 1884, the erstwhile colonizers imperiously created artificial boundaries sometimes dividing an ethnic group among two or more imperial powers. Achebe decried this peremptory acts of the imperial powers in his seminal book of essays, *Morning Yet on Creation Day* (1975:57) thus:

> The country which we know as Nigeria today began not so very long ago as the arbitrary creation of the British. It is true, as William Fagg says in his excellent new book Nigerian Images, that this arbitrary creation has proved as lucky in terms of African art history as any enterprise of the fortunate Prince of Serendip. And I believe that in political and economic terms too this arbitrary creation called Nigeria holds out great prospects. Yet the fact remains that Nigeria was created by the British – for their own ends. Let us give the devil his due: colonialism in Africa disrupted many things, but it did create big political units where there were small scattered ones before. Nigeria had hundreds of autonomous communities ranging in size from the vast Fulani Empire founded by Usman dan Fodio in the North to tiny village entities in the East. Today it is one country. Of course there are areas in Africa where colonialism divided up a single ethnic group among two or even three powers. But on the whole it did bring together many peoples that had hitherto gone their several ways.

What Achebe says about Nigeria in the above excerpt applies virtually to all African countries. Seen in that light, the country we call Cameroon today is an artificial entity created by the colonial powers for their own ends. That explains why over fifty years after the attainment of political independence, Cameroonians are still unable to develop a sense of national unity and identity. It also accounts, as Mazrui (242) puts it, for the "conflict between patriotism and paternity, between allegiance to the nation and loyalty to one's family."

One of the negative consequences of European incursion into Africa was the tribal and other conflicts that ensued. Longue Longue gives a sober description of the situation in his album, "Privatisation" (2003):

> Au temps de nos ancestres, il y avait la paix en Africa oh
> Au temps de nos aieux, il y avait la paix (x2)
> Mais quand les blanc est arrive la guerre a commence
> Quand les colons sont arrive oh la guerre a commence (x2)
> Ils sont venus comme des missionnaires
> Alors qu'ils etaient des mercenaries
> Ils ont pille toutes nos richesses...
> Les Blancs, pour s'installer en Afrique
> Ils ont presente la Bible, Ils ont cree des religions
> Ils ont divise nos parents, ils ont cree des religions
> Ils ont divise nos aieux
> Et quand nos aieux se sont divise oh mama
> La guerre a commence.

> In the days of our ancestors there was peace in Africa oh
> In the days of our ancestors there was peace (x2)
> But, when the whites arrived, war started
> When the colonizers arrived oh, war started (x2)
> They came as missionaries
> While in actual fact they were mercenaries
> They have pillaged all our wealth...
> For the whites to establish themselves in Africa,
> They presented the Bible and created multiple religions
> They divided our parents and created multiple religions
> They divided our ancestors
> And when our ancestors have been disunited oh mama
> War started.

The colonial policies which Longue Longue fustigates led to ethnic consciousness. That is, the ethnic rivalries between the major ethnic groups in post colonial Cameroon started during the colonial period.

Political Corruption and Abuse of Power
Corruption is generally defined as the dishonest use of one's position or power to one's own advantage. But, corruption is also multi-faceted and therefore subject to several interpretations. To Mazrui (242), for example,

> *Corruption is not just a case of receiving favours from outside. It is also a question of misappropriating funds from inside. To some extent, the problem goes back to the colonial administration, with all its rootlessness and lack of legitimacy. The colonial regime was alienated from the population not only because by definition, it was a case of foreign control but also because it was artificial, newly invented. Because the government lacked legitimacy, government property lacked respect.*

Mazrui traces the origin and evolution of corruption in Africa. He claims that Africans under colonial rule had no qualms in stealing from the colonial administration whom they considered in the first place as a foreign thief. Unfortunately, this cynical attitude to government property was carried over into the post-colonial period and eventually led to the entrenchment of nepotism and favouritism in the system. It would appear that A.Y. Andoh (1970:4) was confirming this view especially when he said that a successful politician in a modern African state is regarded as an investment by his tribal group:

> *The wide extension of kinship bonds means that a chief (or any other official) is frequently put into the position of having to choose between his obligations to favour particular kinsmen and his official duty to act disinterestedly. This type of conflict of obligation is quite real for the politician, civil servant, policeman, or even judge. For a successful political candidate is regarded by many of his constituents (frequently his kinsmen) as an investment, and will be asked for jobs or scholarships, or for help in local disputes.*

Emmanuel Wallerstein in (P.C.Loyd, 1967:14) supported this thesis in his essay "Ethnicity and National Integration in West Africa" when he asserts that:

> *The dysfunctional aspects of ethnicity for national integration are obvious. They are basically two. The*

> *first is that ethnic groups are still particularistic in their orientation and diffuse in their obligation, even if they are less so than the extended family. The ethnic roles are insufficiently segregated from the occupational and political roles because of the extensiveness of the ethnic group. Hence we have the resulting familiar problems of nepotism and corruption.*

Here, then, lies the origin of the corruption, graft, tribalistic patronage, chicanery and the undermining of such democratic principles as accountability, meritocracy, and the freedom of expression which post-colonial Cameroon and most independent African nations are afflicted with. As Mazrui (240) explained,

> *Politics in Africa, for example, are sometimes hard to keep clean merely because people are moving from one set of values to another. In no other area of life is this better illustrated than in the issue of ethnic solidarity and kinship obligations. Pressures are exerted on an African official or politician to remind him of those who shared his social womb. People from his area or from his clan enquire how best the well-placed African politician, or even academic, might help his kinsmen to gain admission to a job or to a scholarship.*

The situation in Cameroon is even more harrowing. Corruption inevitably led to under-development, poverty, and misery that, in turn, tended towards unrest and instability. This is how Francis B. Nyamnjoh describes the Cameroonian predicament in his fiery article "Cameroon: A Country United by Ethnic Ambition and Difference" (1999:109):

> *The power elite becomes obsessed with maximizing power at ethnic or, while treating the centre as sacrosanct. The minister or general manager from the North-West or South-West is made to understand that he owes his appointment to the dis-appointment of another Anglophone, and that he must derail all signs of solidarity among Anglophones, regardless of province of origin, if he counts on staying in office. Thus, it is not uncommon to find CPDM barons of the North-West Province condemning South-Westerners without distinction, and vice versa. Appointing an Anglophone Prime Minister is hardly hailed as the regime's*

recognition of Anglophones in general, but rather, as a victory for North-Westerners or South-Westerners as the case may be. The same is true of ministers whose first visits after appointment are usually to their home village to muster support and/or gratitude for the centre, as well as to prove that they have a power base of some sort. This also reveals that they are first and foremost ministers for their ethnic group, before being ministers for Cameroon as a whole, if at all. The system produces trouble-makers, and this include promoting inter-provincial or inter-ethnic conflicts, which the central government regulates and crushes from time to time when things get a little out of hand.

It is this dirty politics and all that it entails that the protest musicians decry. This is seen in Lapiro de Mbanga's song "Lefam So" (2001):

Fo insai dis situation fo favoritism ana nepotisme all man don ton na boukateur...
Riguer et moralization yes now na rancoeur et marginalization
Pour le liberalism communautaire don ton na pour la liberalism de corruption.
We di evolue now for regime de tchoko and institutionalization de faux...
Yes now, na tchop a tchop
Tresorier payeur, percepteur ana fonde de pouvoir dem bout de signature na 30%
Medecins, infirmiers and aides- soignnants weti circuit na zero tchoko zero soins.
Gangsters weti anti-gangs na cohabitation pacifique.
Taximen, les mototaxis et le transporteurs dem de fo corps a corps weti mbere.
Agents de peage routier, dem di cut two cents dans le easy.

In this context of favouritism and nepotism, we have all become a bunch of dishonest persons and crooks.
Rigour and moralization have been transformed into resentment and marginalization.
Communal liberalism has become liberalism of corruption.

> We are now evolving in a system of corruption and fraud.
> Now, it is a matter of eat-and-let-eat.
> The signatures of the government treasurer and paymaster cost a cool 30%.
> Doctors, nurses, midwives, and nursing- aids have established a rule of no bribe no treatment.
> Racketeers and members of the criminal squad cohabit peacefully.
> Taxi drivers, motorcycle riders and public transporters rub shoulders with policemen
> Toll gate collectors deduct two, two hundred francs from road users without qualms.

In the above song, Lapiro excoriates against bribery and corruption which take several forms and pervade every aspect of life in Cameroon. This is in line with Nyamnjoh's (112) view on the subject:

> The culture of corruption cuts across the entire society. Everyone is doing it at his own level, from top to bottom – the only difference being that those at the top have more to steal from, they are stealing and making off with a lot more. In a way, Cameroonians all have an interest in maintaining the status quo: from the taximan and the police or gendarme officer at the check-point, to the parent and college principal during admissions, the customs inspector and the businessman at the port, the civil servant chasing files at the ministry, the university lecturer trading marks for sex and cash, etc., right up to the helm of the state. Because they each have a bit of the system in them (either through direct involvement with the centre or via links of patronage and influence) and thus a vested interest. It becomes very difficult to contemplate the system's undoing without in a way contemplating one's very own undoing.

Recruitment and promotion of Cameroonians is often based on whom you know rather than what you know. As Nyamnjoh (107) puts it,

> The system has little regard for virtue and meritocracy and proves to have more room for loyal mediocrity than critical excellence. It thrives on appearances and not on substance, making subservient mediocrities feel more

important than real achievers, hence the omnipresence of: 'savez-vous a qui vous avez affaire?' A second- or third-rate academic, for example, who provides the regime with the conceptual rhetoric it needs to justify its excesses and highhandedness, is more likely to be promoted to professor (with or without publications) and made dean, vice-chancellor or even minister, and to accumulate portfolios, than his more productive but critical counterpart who is denied promotion and recognition for being a genuine intellectual.

This is exactly what Lapiro is lambasting the system for:

Ma complices dem don learn buk sote dem get diplome
But dem no de for pays organisateur, dem go do how now?
Dem don lance concours na da so tchoko jam.
If you no de fo equipe national, you go do how now?

My friends have gone to school and obtained certificates,
But since they do not know anybody in position of authority what can they do?
Competitive examinations have been launched, but there is no money to bribe the authorities.
If you don't know one of the leaders, you are helpless.

The Pathological Greed of the Privileged and the Mighty

The artists are particularly concerned with the gargantuan social disequilibrium aggravated by the privileged few who are drawn from the highest echelons of society and who are already swimming in scandalous opulence. Lapiro lashes out against those in positions of power for their self-seeking propagation of tribalism, ethnicism, and squandermania in "Lefam So":

Big Katika for Ngola anayi Nchinda
Dem don cash all dan mbourou.
Dem yan kan kan buk for tapis and dem tie
Chateaux fo sai bai sai au vu et su de tous
Ignorant avec mepris, arrogance et insolence
Ndoutou fo their condre pipi.

> *The President of Ngola (Yaounde) and his ministers*
> *Have appropriated everything.*
> *They buy all makes of cars, build mansions all over the Republic.*
> *Ignoring the poverty and misery of their people.*

He continues in another song, "Qui n'est rien n'a rien to state that power relations in Cameroon are maintained economically and politically:

> *You na who no mola?*
> *Na members dem fo tchop pipi their money ana all complices dem helep all things for Mboko yard.*
> *All societies na dem own.*
> *Gagner credit ou marches na so so dem.*
> *Na fait fo bien execute dat their own eglise weh I de for render definitivement pauvres les citoyens.*
> *President du conseil d"administration na dem.*
> *President directeur general na dem, administration na so so dem.*
> *Actionnaires majoritaires na dem, actionnaires minoritaires na dem.*
> *Doh fo kerosene and pipeline na dem di damme.*
> *Doh fo timber ana all kind kind sitik na anaconda di swallowam.*
> *Gold, diamant, alluminium na soso dem.*
>
> *You, who are you, my friend?*
> *Only those who embezzle the country's wealth are friends.*
> *They own everything in this country.*
> *All the companies belong to them.*
> *All the contracts and kick-backs are controlled by them.*
> *It seems as if they belong to a cult whose main objective is to perpetuate the poverty of the small people.*
> *They are Presidents of Administrative Councils.*
> *The General Managers and Administrators are still them.*
> *They hold both the majority and minority shares in State Corporations.*
> *They are the ones who squander the money from petrol.*
> *They gobble up the income from timber and forest exploitation.*

> *Gold, diamond and aluminum are firmly in their grip.*

Lapiro is in effect saying that there is no social justice, equity and fair play in the distribution of the wealth of the nation because members of the ruling class in the political and economic sectors as well as in the civil service have appropriated everything. Lapiro's vituperations are likely to lead his audience to ask two questions: Firstly, what is the nation, Cameroon for? That is, what does Cameroon mean to those at the centre and those at the margins? And, secondly, are the two classes of Cameroonians bound by a common sense of belonging and purpose? Nyamnjoh (111) proposes the following answers:

> *Sometimes one can understand the cynicism of those who think that most Cameroonians in high office or business see their country essentially in terms of a natural plantation. Their dreams of power do not seem to go further than having a place at the dining table, and benefiting from what a minister under Ahidjo once referred to as : "les gratitude et les servitudes de la function publique." Their struggle in the name of democracy seem more like the war of the bellies where the 'eaters' ('les buffeurs') are questioned, but seldom the act of 'eating' ('bouffer'). Patrons and clients may be questioned, but not patronage and patrimonialism. To many people in or seeking high office, Cameroon is little more than a farm tended by God but harvested by man.*

Exploitation and Oppression of the Masses

I am using the term "masses" here to refer to the victims of the depredation of oppressive power who have been forced by the present state of affairs in the country to live on the fringes of society. They are the low income workers, the uneducated, the unemployed, the hawkers and other underprivileged members of the society. Their common denominator is that they are "caught between then anvil and the hammer". There is no doubt that this underprivileged class of Cameroonians want a change for the better. "They want to have an active say in matters of public interest, and to free themselves from the misery of which they are victims". But they have been emasculated to the point of being silenced. As Nyamnjoh (116) observes,

> *The masses are passive spectators in decision-making at many levels, perhaps because they have relied overmuch on politicians and elites, rather than on their own ability to organize themselves into social forces with a contribution to make. Political affairs and social life are not organized and conducted in a way that allow for effective access to decision-making for all and sundry, and for an equitable distribution of the fruits of progress among the various social groups.*

Lapiro sings about the marginalization, exploitation, and rejection of these small people. He makes their welfare the centre of his ideology in his masterpiece and best-selling album "Mimba We". This song is pregnant with meaning. Firstly, it is a clarion call on the affluent political vultures, that is, the state officials who have selfishly appropriated the scarce resources of the nation to remember the downtrodden who are wallowing in abject poverty when it comes to the sharing of the national cake. Secondly, it is a sober reminder that the "petit people" who constitute an important segment of the Cameroonian population have been marginalized, rejected, and ignored by a comprador minority. Thirdly, it is an open recognition of the fact that those who wield political power in the country have deliberately refused to provide opportunities for individual and collective fulfillment of those who legitimize their power. Finally, the title "Mimba We" points to the overt subject of the song which, put quite simply, is that it is only by responding effectively to the aspirations of the common people that peace, progress and development can be assured. Thus, "Mimba We" is a fervent call from those on the periphery of society to those at the centre to remember them by creating a society where the rulers and the ruled can live in harmony and where peace and progress can prevail. Lapiro elaborates on the above subjects in the following lines:

    Lapiro: You wan dame you mimba we
              You wan sule you mimba we

> *You wan nyoxer you mimba we*
> *Oh mimba we ooh*
> Chorus: *Oh mimba we*

> Lapiro: *When you want to eat, you should think of us.*
> *When you want to drink, you should think of us*
> *When you want to have sex, you should think of us*
> *Oh think of us.*
> Chorus: *Oh think of us.*

The above passage is a desperate appeal to those in positions of power who have been desensitized to the corruption and abuse around them not to continue to turn a blind eye to the predicament of the masses. Lapiro goes on to allude to the dilemma of the underprivileged majority who lack such basic necessities of life like simple shelter, food and clean drinking water but who do not want to be pushed into using unorthodox means to obtain them.

> Lapiro: *Weti we go dame?*
> *Weti we go sule?*
> *Oh oh?*
> Chorus: *Na fo wusai we go nang oh?*
> Lapiro: *We no wan kik oh*
> *We no wan go fo ngata*
> *We de da so fo ndembre*
> *I beg mimba we ooh...yes.*
> *We no wan problem tara*
> *We no wan go kondengui*
> *We de find daso garri*
> *For helep we own family oh...*

> Lapiro: *What shall we eat?*
> *What shall we drink?*
> *Eh....*
> Chorus: *Where shall we sleep?*
> Lapiro: *We don't want to steal, big brother,*
> *We don't want to be imprisoned*
> *We are only out to hustle*
> *Please think of us too.*
> *We don't want to pick pockets*
> *We don't want to go to Kondengui (maximum security prison)*

> We are merely looking for daily bread for our families.

Lapiro is here anticipating and warning. He is beating the battle drum summoning his people to join him in taking up verbal arms against the oppressors. Nevertheless, like most crusaders, Lapiro is naturally anxious to know if the people on whose behalf he is staking his life are solidly behind him. So he uses a call and response pattern to find out. Their resounding response is an indication that he has succeeded in rousing and holding their attention.

Lapiro:	Nkouloulou I wan tok!
	Mokolo I wan give dictee
	Gare routier a masham?
	Marche central I go troway,
	Sauveteur, I chakara?
Chorus:	Go bifo, go bifo, go bifo.
	Motion, motion, motion.
	Ndinga man no swa,
	All complice dem de for your back, Tara.
:Lapiro:	Nkouloulou I want to say something
	Mokolo I want to decree
	Motor park should I smash it?
	Central market I will spill it
	Street vendors should I scatter things?
Chorus:	Go ahead, go ahead, go ahead.
	Motions, Motions, Motions.
	Ndinga man don't panic
	All your comrades in arms are behind you, big shot.

The questions and answers underline the central essence and ideological foundation of the economic structure of Cameroon. The term "my people" as used by Lapiro is inclusive as well as exclusive. It distinguishes those at the base who belong from those at the superstructure who do not belong. If you are at the base then you are tied to all those at the base of society by bonds of a common belonging. You are subject to the laws of the base because you have a stake in the struggle for the improvement of the well-being of all those at the base of the society. Hence, with the support and encouragement of his incensed comrades in arms, Lapiro plunges into a full diatribe against the excesses of an insensitive government.

Lapiro: O.K. Mola, no bi da so fo secteur for Peter Botha
We I bad eh,
Moyen no de for Ngola.
Repe fo sai fo iton don beke,
Yes, Jacques Chirac for Ngola
Don komot corige fo ultimatum.
He say ma own pipi dem musi dame shutun.
Ehem, he say sauveteurs dem musi yung.
Dem de bumbla ma complices dem sai bai sai.
Na dem dat for mboko
Moyen fo dame no de
Mburu for pay locations sep nating.
Ngiri don make reme ana njanga
Dem don dry leke enchantillon for Ethiopia.
A man, sauveteur na boulouh wey
I no get compression du personnel,
Sauvetage na boulouh wey I no get retrait anticipe
Fo we own boulouh fo sauvetage,
Dem no de ask man diplome ana cinq ans d'experience.
Fo sauvetage, I'l n'ya pas de concours.
Ehe, lef me a truwe Francais i don bad.
We wey we noba get ntong for go sukul fo sai for Ngoa-ekele
Na fo sauvetage we de find we own garri.

O.K. Mola (uncle), it is not only in Peter Botha's country that things have gone awry.
There are no means of survival in Yaounde.
The father of the country is irked.
Yes, the Jacques Chirac of Yaounde has issued an ultimatum.
He says that my cohorts should eat stones.
He says that my supporters should perish.
My accomplices are being harassed everywhere.
There they are in the country with no means to fend for themselves.
No money to pay house rents.

> Hardship has made mothers and their children to be as haggard as the famine stricken people of Ethiopia.
> My friend, hustling is an activity that does not lead to lay-offs.
> Hustling is an activity that does not lead to early retirement.
> Our hustling activities do not require diplomas or Five years working experience.
> To be a hustler, you do not need to pass an entrance examination.
> Ehe, let me speak in French. Things have gone off-hand.
> We who are not so fortunate to go to school in Ngoa-ekele
> It is through hustling that we can fend for ourselves.

The above excerpt reflects Lapiro's intense disillusionment with the way things are going in Cameroon. It is also a serious indictment of the political leadership's consolidation of power and autocratic rule.

After castigating the calculated ruthlessness, brazen selfishness, and blatant unscrupulousness of the ruling class, the outspoken musician turns his artistic searchlight on the economic crisis, a canker worm, which is at the root of the socio-economic muddle, and large-scale misery in which Cameroon finds itself.

> *For dis heure for austerite so, a man,*
> *For dis heure wey cinq no musi change position,*
> *Yes, austerite da bi say dolla no musi change foot,*
> *Wusai we own espoir de now?*
> *Me a mimba say na time dis way*
> *All man musi dembre for yi own secteur,*
> *For say make we bumbla dan cris economique,*
> *Way yi don put all man a genou.*

At this hour of austerity, my friend
At this hour when a dime must not be displaced.
Yes, austerity means that a dollar must not be substituted.
Where then is our hope?
I thought that the time is ripe

> For everyone to work in his domain to fight this economic crisis
> That has overwhelmed everyone.

The vocal critic of the Government expresses his bitter disappointment at the fact that Cameroonians have abdicated their responsibility for fighting the economic crisis which has thus been given free rein to engulf the whole country. Lapiro then turns his attention to the whole business of national unity and national integration which he sees as a smokescreen sustained to frustrate attempts at positive change.

> *Integration nationale na weti noh?*
> *Na say dem musi rafla ara pipi?*
> *Or na say all we musi put hand say make we helep*
> *We own don grand for Etoudi fo boulouh?*
> *Jes now if you get bacalo-licence oh, you go*
> *Boulouh for wusai?*
> *D'ailleur sep njoh pajero and njoh Mercedes yi don bolle.*
> *So now, a man, we de beg daso,*
> *Wi taximan, wi bi sauveteurs dem*
> *Wi na pipi for chuk head.*
> *Repe no de, Reme no de.*
> *Lef wi make we helep wi own skin.*
>
> *What is this so-called national integration?*
> *Does it mean that we should exclude others from our common heritage?*
> *Or does it mean that we should unite and help our perplexed President?*
> *Right now even if you hold a bacalo-licence where shall you find work?*
> *Anyway, the era of free pajeros and free Mercedes is gone.*
> *So, Mr. President, we are only pleading.*
> *We are just taximen, mere scrappers.*
> *Managing to eke out a living.*
> *We have no fathers and no mothers.*
> *Please give us a chance to help ourselves.*

The rhetorical questions raised by Lapiro in the above excerpt clarify certain pertinent issues. Instead of helping to consolidate national unity and give the people a sense of national identity, the so-called national integration has set off a degenerative process: freedom has become corruption and democracy has collapsed into autocracy. Lapiro concludes his fiery diatribe against inept political leadership by pleading that the common people should be allowed to participate in political discussions and decisions. The point must however be made here that Lapiro is not seeking change for the sake of change. Rather he is seeking the change that will improve the human condition and develop Cameroon's human resources.

In "Mimba We", Lapiro focuses on the informal sector. Since employment in the formal sector has become almost an impossibility, the unemployed youths have found alternative jobs in the informal sector. They have taken to selling second hand clothing, operating phone booths, pushing trucks, carrying passengers on motor cycles, selling fruits at street corners and doing all kinds of odd jobs in order to keep body and soul together. But, in Yaounde, Douala, and other big towns, the Municipal Councils are at war with this class of marginalized Cameroonians, driving them away from the streets ostensibly in an attempt to keep the towns clean. It was Lapiro's virulent and fiery crusading songs that prompted the City Councils to stop harassing the hawkers. This is a clear indication that Lapiro is in direct touch with the ordinary Cameroonians. It also testifies to the efficacy of protest songs. As a result of his victory over the Government Delegates, the "sauveteurs" and "debroillards" appreciate Lapiro and hail him as their uncontested leader, their "big Katika". Another success, this time scored by Lapiro and other protest musicians, is that the Government has, at last, decided to organize the informal sector, and to create space around the main markets for the vendors. It is to be hoped that this is the beginning of the long awaited change for the better.

Power Alternation
Power alternation is an important feature of democracy. It helps, among other things, to prevent the monopoly of state power by an individual or a hegemonic party system, it

strengthens the nation, and it reduces tensions and conflicts between the different groups over power and leadership. But, the tendency among power incumbents in contemporary African countries, from the perspective of the protest artists, is to cling to power at all cost. This is in direct contradiction to the wishes of the population who expect to see a smooth and democratic transfer of power in their respective countries at regular constitutional intervals.

It is however a known fact that "no human being voluntarily surrenders power in the absence of constraints". These constraints, according to political analysts are the constitution, the electoral system, and the party system which must function in tandem. But this tripod for power alternation are easily circumvented or revoked by "sit-tight" African leaders, thus generating discontent among the population and making the question of alternation in state leadership the principal source of political unrest in contemporary Africa.

The Cameroon story is a case in point. It will be recalled that the country gained political independence in 1960. Since then, it has had only two Heads of State: Ahmadou Ahidjo who ruled for 22 years from 1960 to 1982; and Paul Biya who took over in 1982 and is still in power. There is no doubt that his reign is more humane and far better than that of his predecessor. Nevertheless, the protest artists are worried by his predilection for revising the constitution. His latest revision in 2007 which effectively removed the presidential term limits sparked off anti-government riots. Lapiro has made that the central theme of his album, "Constitution Constipee" which he released in 2007. The album was banned just two months after it was released. It is widely believed that the release of that album eventually led to his arrest and imprisonment. The album opens with the following lines:

Constitution a gauche, constitution a droite,
Revision en haut, revision en bas,
Motion de soutien par ci, contre motion par la,
Marche de soutien le jour, contre marche la nuit.
Levez les mains, levez les mains x4

Constitution by the left, constitution by the right.

> *Revision up there, revision down here.*
> *Motions of support here, motions of support there.*
> *Support rallies by day, counter rallies by night.*
> *Raise your hands, raise your hands, x4*

Lapiro opens his song with the equivocation that characterizes politics in order to highlight the confusion that surrounds Cameroonian politics. Nyamnjoh (113) shares the views of Lapiro that by constantly changing the constitution in search of perfection, the political leadership is leaving the substance for the shadow:

> *But what I believe is that one can have the greatest blueprint on paper, but when people disregard with impunity laws which they themselves have voted saying that laws are made by man and need not be applied to the letter, what use is a perfect constitution? Our greatest problem is not the lack of law, nor is it a problem of imperfect laws. The simple truth is that Cameroon is yet to be imbued with a sense of mission or purpose as a country. To what extent this lack of vision can be explained by the bloody crushing of radical nationalism in Cameroon before and after independence, has already been contemplated by some historians and political scientists.*

It is this chronic lack of vision that irks Lapiro and leads him to train his searchlight on the Head of State himself but addresses him using circumlocution:

> *Liberez Big Katika, liberez repe ndos!*
> *Le pate est fatigue, foutez-lui la paix!*
> *Liberez Big Katika, liberez repe ndos!*
> *Le pacho est tire oh, foutez lui la paix.*

> *Free the boss, free the carefree father.*
> *The old man is tired, let him take a rest.*
> *Free the old man, free the carefree father.*
> *That man is tired o, let him take a rest.*

Lapiro is indirectly reminding the Head of State that age is catching up with him and that he needs to take a well-deserved rest. In other words, he should relinquish his claim to the presidency. He then launches into a long diatribe against the entire political leadership:

A vrai dire, après 15 ans de gabegie,
Est-ce que something fit changer?
Donc, how wi equipe nouvelle fo long crayon,
Their own government go be o, better dem lefam so,
Sans diplome too dem try.
So nor, ba professeurs agreges, ba Dr. d'Etat oh, ba ingenieurs
Weti cravat, avec bureau climatises ooo.
Wuna lef les autres petits diplomes, wuna lefam so!
Lefam so so, lefam so x4
Bo a say you lefam so.
Lefam so, lefam so.
Douala say essele ninka,
Lefam so lefam so.
Bafoussam say takneng takneng,
Lefam so lefam so.
Bamenda say lefam so,
Lefam so lefam so.
Maroua say laisse comme ca,
Lefam so lefam so.
Garoua say ca suffit,
Lefam so lefam so.
Ngaoundere say y en a assez
Lefam so lefam so.
Nkonsamba sya I don bad oo

Truly speaking, after fifteen years of quagmire,
Can anything change?
Therefore, in the impossibility of assessing the output of the new team of bureaucrats and technocrats,
It is better for them to leave the scene.
Let the less educated also try.
Consequently, holders of the aggregation, doctorates, engineers
With ties and air-conditioned offices,
Please allow the less educated, give them a chance.
Leave it like that x4
My friend, I entreat you to leave it like that.
Douala says leave it like that.
Resign and leave it.
Bafoussam says leave it like that.
Resign and leave it.

> *Bamenda says leave it like that.*
> *Resign and leave it.*
> *Maroua says leave it like that.*
> *Resign and leave it.*
> *Garoua says leave it like that,*
> *Resign and leave it.*
> *Ngaoundere says leave it like that.*
> *Resign and leave it.*
> *Nkongsamba says leave it like that.*
> *Resign and leave it.*

Lapiro is in effect saying that the present regime has had its day and should give way to others too to try. He then indicts the educated elite for their collusion with corrupt political officials, and their own involvement with corruption. He goes further to argue that since they, as intellectuals have failed, they should cede their places to the less qualified who remain the only hope of the society. Finally, his listing of the principal towns of the country is another way of saying that the entire country is fed up with the excesses of the regime and would want it to hand over power constitutionally.

Lapiro is not the only artist who is angry with the constant revision of the national constitution by the political leadership. Longue Longue is even more inflammatory and virulent in his criticism of what he sees as the Machiavellian machinations of the nation's grave diggers in "Maladie d'Afrique":

> *Ayo eh Longue Longue Jass*
> *Je suis votre liberateur.*
> *Je vais mourir pour vous, Cinquante ans au pouvoir.*
> *C'est ca la maladie*
> *De l'Afrique.*
> *C'est faire success devant ses enfants c'est ca la maladie de l'Afrique.*
> *C'est ca le virus Ngono lique, c'est ca la maladie de l'Afrique.*
> *Daniel Georgia animatrice Yaounde*
> *Detourner les fonds publique c'est ca la l'Afrique*
> *Epargner a l'etranger, c'est ca la maladie de l'Afrique*
> *Ils nous gerent comme de betail*
> *Ils nou dirigent comme les aveugles oh*

Ils ne respecte pas le people ye ye oh oh.
On ne veut plus ca oh oh.
Laisser vos chateau et vos merkos essayez vous verrez.
Essayer vous verrez que le pays va mal
Essayez vous verrez la souffrance...
Hier tout le pays c'est ca...
Truquer les election c'est ca...
Changer la constitution, c'est ca...
Ils changent la constitution x2
Comme ils veulent et quant ils veulent.
Essayez vous verrez
Que nous somme pas des Togolais, essayez vous verrez.
Que nous somme pas des Congolais, essayez vous verrez
Que nous somme pas Bourkinabes, essayez vous verrez
Que nous somme pas aveugles, ye ye ye essayez vous verrez.
Nous somme Camerounais essayez vous verrez.
J. Remy Ngono, ils ont garantie leur avenir chez le blanc.
Ils ont construis des chateaux la bas chez les blancs
Ils ont meme des enterprises oh la bas chez les blancs
Ils on meme des doubles nationalite la bas chez les blancs.
Nous laissant dans la pauvrette, on ne veut plus ca oh oh
En laissant le pays dans le chomage....

Ayo eh Longue Longue Jass
I am your liberator, I will die for you.
Fifty years in power. That is Africa's illness
Displaying success to their children, that is Africa's illness
That is the Ngono league virus, that is Africa,s illness
Daniel Georgia, Animator in Yaounde
Embezzling public funds, that is Africa
Saving in foreign banks, that is Africa's illness
They rule us like cattle
They lead us like the blind oh
They have no respect for anyone ye ye oh oh
We do not want that any more oh

> *Leave your castles and Mercedes benz cars, try and you will see*
> *Try and you will see that the country is sick*
> *Try and you will experience the suffering*
> *Try and you will see x4*
> *Fifty years in power, that is the illness*
> *Yesterday, the whole country was like that*
> *Rigging of elections that is it*
> *Revising the constitution, that is it*
> *They revise the constitution x2*
> *How they want and*
> *When they want*
> *Try and you will see*
> *That we are not Togolese, try and you will see*
> *That we are not Congolese, try and you will see*
> *That we are not burkinabes*
> *That we are not blind ye ye ye try and you will see*
> *That we are Cameroonians, try and you will see*
> *J. Remy Ngono, they have secured their future in the white man's country*
> *They have built castles there in the white man's land*
> *They even own businesses in the white man's country*
> *They even have double nationalities in the white man's country*
> *Abandoning us in abject poverty. We will not stomach that anymore*
> *Leaving his countrymen unemployed.*

Longue longue begins his harangue by declaring himself as the liberator of his people and, knowing that he runs the risk of being apprehended, he quickly declares his willingness to die for the cause of his people. He then delves into the heart of the matter. He calls into question the penchant of leaders to stay in power, their propensity for revising the constitution, their proclivity to embezzle public funds, and their tendency to forget the people they govern. It is in these circumstances that longue Longue calls for a democratic change of leadership.

In conclusion, it can be said that the artists whose songs have been analysed in this chapter presume that since the politicians and intellectuals have lost touch with the realities of the people's existence and problems; since they are unable to correct the excesses and muddles which they have themselves created; and since they lack the goodwill and genuine commitment to democracy, good governance, and to promoting the collective aspirations of the people for stability, peace, and orderly development, they are unfit to govern and should leave power to the common people. However, the artists hardly allude to the endemic weakness of the civil society, and the apathy and cynicism of the impoverished and dispossessed people. Hence it is difficult to say whether the artists actually think that the disaffected masses have the means of effecting the positive changes they yearn for. Whatever the case, one thing is clear and that is, that Cameroonians still have some waiting to do before they see the light at the end of the tunnel.

CHAPTER FOUR
THE POLITICAL ECONOMY OF DEPENDENCY

> *The kind of capitalism which was transferred to Africa was itself shallow. Western consumption patterns were transferred more effectively than Western production techniques. Western tastes were acquired more quickly than Western skills, the profit motive was adopted without the efficient calculus of entrepreneurship, and capitalist greed was internalized sooner than capitalist discipline (Mazrui, 14).*

In the introductory chapter of this book, I made the point that the Cameroonian economy is still predominantly agricultural and firmly controlled by Western multi-nationals and mega corporations. In this chapter, I intend to examine what the protest musicians see as the reasons why Cameroon's efforts at development and modernization are stultified and why in economic terms the country is becoming marginal to world industrial development and global commerce. The reasons given by the protest musicians are many but, for the purposes of this chapter, I shall limit myself to political mismanagement, collusion with the erstwhile colonial masters to milk the nation dry, economic exploitation, the heavy debt burden, privatization of public enterprises and, above all, the breakdown of morality.

Political Mismanagement
As a consequence of the political mismanagement of the country by leaders who have the predilection of seeing the country in terms of a farm which should be plundered at will, several things went wrong. The most important was the economic crises that triggered a chain reaction. The Franc CFA was devalued, and that precipitated a significant curtailment in the salaries of civil servants, massive retrenchments in the work force, and the consequent drop in the purchasing power of Cameroonians. To complicate matters, Cameroon was declared the most corrupt country in the world by

Transparency International. Bouki Solo in "40 temps de Pouvoir" (2003) anathemizes against the predatory attitude of the people in power who have become desensitized to the corruption and abuse of power going on around them:

> *Depuis l'independence, rien n'a change*
> *On recule, on n'avance pas.*
> *Le dirigeants ne s'inquitent pas.*
> *Les people pleure, les people peut crever.*
> *Il faut qu'ils (parlant des dirigeants) ecoutent.*
> *Avec l'argent du diamante construisez-nous des routes.*
> *Avec l'argent du petrole donnez-nous la lumiere.*
> *Avec l'argent du bois creez-nous des emploi.*
> *Au lieu de construire des chateaux qui vous n'habiterez jamais,*
> *Au lieu d'acheter les armes pour vous maintenir au pouvoir,*
> *Trop de galere en Afrique...*
> *L'avenir des jeunes est hypotheque...*
> *Debout la generation consciente doit se reveiller*
> *Changer de mentalite.*

> *Since independence nothing has changed.*
> *We regress, we do not make progress.*
> *The leaders are not bothered.*
> *The people are crying, they may soon break down.*
> *It is necessary for the leaders to listen.*
> *With money from the sale of diamond construct roads for us.*
> *With money from the sale of petrol provide electricity for us.*
> *With money from the sale of timber, create jobs for us.*
> *Instead of building castles in which you will never live,*
> *Instead of buying arms to maintain yourselves in power,*
> *Too much mess in Africa.*
> *The future of our youths has been mortgaged.*
> *Stand up. The conscious generation must wake up.*
> *Change your mentality.*

Solo blames the failure of the system on the materialistic individualism that is seen in the conspicuous consumption of the privileged class who build castles in which they will never live, and buy arms with which to consolidate their hold on power. The artist blames the leaders for ignoring the suffering masses, but he still pleads with them to use the money from the sale of the country's natural resources for the development of the country instead of squandering it on useless projects.

Foreign Debt Servicing
The musicians censure the Bretton Woods Institutions – the World Bank and the International Monetary Fund (IMF) who impose stiff economic and austerity measures on Cameroon thereby debilitating the already fragile economy. These capitalist institutions then loan huge sums of money to the country at prohibitive interest rates. Unable to repay the colossal debt, Cameroon is left with no choice but to continue to service the huge debt and to negotiate conditions for rescheduling it. Lapiro presents the situation graphically in "Lefam So":

>Dis can na sick weh my contri de sick a noba siyam.
>Dis can na sick weh my contri de sick I no get meresine.
>Il n'y a vraiment pas de soins, sometime na fever,
>Some time na ebola, a no no mi.
>Some time na ballok, man no fit sabi,
>Ballok weh big repe he don lefam for wi.
>Dis can na sick weh Cameroun di sick a noba siyam,
>La il n'y a vraiment pas remede.
>Banque Mondial don make kind kind consultation,
>Bretton Woods don write all kind ordonnance,
>Club de Paris don vaccine.
>FMI don put perfusion with accord de confirmation.
>Premiere accord, deuxieme accord, troisieme accord,
>Quatrieme accord de confirmation.
>Ou est le bout du tunnel?...
>Pourtant Banque Mondiale, FMI, le Club de Paris a na all structures financiers dem don touch wi doh avec majoration.
>Credit remboursable dans cent ans plus les annees de reechelonnement.
>Dat mean say djanga fo we djanga dem go come bolo fo pay dam doh.
>Donc non seulement popo wi sep sep wi don ton ninga,

We don bate hypotheque l'avenir fo we muna fo ever and ever...
Au fait mi a di askam se, popo dan credit weh wi di pay Chaque jour, yi montant na combien?
Wi bin don pay combien ana I di jam combien?
No man no sabi.

This kind of illness that my country is suffering from I have never seen it.
This kind of illness that my country is suffering has no known cure.
There is really no known cure, maybe it is fever, maybe it is ebola, I don't know.
Perhaps it is ill-luck which our grand comrade has bequeath to us.
This kind of illness that Cameroon is suffering from, I have never seen it.
There is no known cure.
The World Bank has carried out all kinds of diagnosis,
Bretton Woods have given prescriptions,
The Club of Paris has even inoculated us against this strange disease.
The IMF has given us drips with confirmation agreements.
First agreement, second agreement, third agreement of confirmation.
Where is the end of the tunnel?
Whereas the World Bank, the International Monetary Fund,
The Club of Paris and all the major financial institutions have given us loans with high interests.
Loans refundable in one hundred years plus the years of rescheduling.
Which means that our children and grand children
Will have to work very hard to repay the loans.
That also presupposes that even we ourselves have been enslaved.
We have mortgaged the future of our off springs forever.
By the way, I want to know the amount of the loans
That we are paying every day?
How much have we repaid and how much is outstanding?

No one appears to know.

In the above song, Lapiro advances the view that the economic policies and austerity measures which the international funding institutions have prescribed for Cameroon with the intention of salvaging the country from the brink of economic collapse – massive deregulation, privatization of public enterprises, Structural Adjustment Plans, export driven strategies and the Heavily Indebted Poor Country Initiative – are the very policies and measures that are being used by the super powers to siphon the limited national resources into foreign debt repayment. The implication here is that these measures have adverse effects on such essential social services as health, education, and infrastructure. Under the circumstances, Lapiro believes that we are left with no alternative than to mortgage the development of our country and the future of our children and grand children.

Privatization of Public Enterprises
The international financial institutions coerced Cameroon into privatizing all the key state owned companies under the guise of encouraging the private sector to fulfil its role as the catalyst of economic development. But in so doing, they have removed one of the principal sources of the country's income from the hands of the government. In order to achieve their objectives they connived with the people in power. As Longue Longue puts it in his song, "Privatisation":

>*Ils nous ont envoyer la conjuncture, on a supporte*
>*Ils nous ont envoyer la crise economique, on a su gerer*
>*Ils nou ont verse les maladies ont s'est preserve oh*
>*Aujourd'hui ils font complicite*
>*Avec nos dirigeants Africains*
>*Pour privatiser nos societies*
>*Nous envoyer au chomage*
>*Ils nous envoient a la mort.*

>*They sent us an unfavorable political situation, we endured it.*
>*They sent us economic crisis, we managed it.*

> *They poured illnesses on us, we persevered.*
> *Today, they enter into complicity*
> *With our African leaders*
> *To privatize our national companies*
> *So as to make us redundant*
> *Thereby sending us to our early graves.*

Having used us against ourselves, the Western powers now have their way to do what they want with our economy. As Longue Longue puts it,

> *Bana la Camair*
> *Privatisee oh, privatisee*
> *La SONEL oh*
> *Privatisee oh, privatisee*
> *Bana la SNEC oh*
> *Privatisee oh ,privatisee*
> *La CAMRAIL*
> *Privatisee oh, privatisee*
> *L'Aeroport de Nsimalen,*
> *Privatisee oh, privatisee*
> *CAMAIR*
> *Privatize oh, privatize*
> *SONEL*
> *Privatize oh, privatize*
> *SNEC*
> *Privatize oh, privatize*
> *CAMRAIL*
> *Privatize oh, privatize*
> *The Nsimalen International Airport*
> *Privatize oh, privatize.*

These state corporations: CAMAIR (Cameroon Airlines), SONEL, (Electricity Corporation), SNEC (Water Corporation), CAMRAIL (Cameroon Railway Corporation) are all key national companies. They provided employments for thousands of Cameroonians, they generated a substantial part of the national budget, and they were the pride of the country. To privatize them therefore is not only to weaken the already fragile economy of the country, but also to transfer the country's wealth into a few foreign hands, and to deal a death blow on the national ego. That is why Longue Longue posed the following pertinent questions:

> *Si vous privatiser nos societies*
> *Qu'allons nous faire eh?*
> *Qu'allons nous faire?*
>
> If you privatize all our national companies
> What are we going to do eh?
> What are we going to do?

These are questions to which neither the neo-colonialists nor the comprador leaders have ready answers. That is why the artist gives the following stern warning.

> *Ne privatisee pas le palais d'Etoudi*
> *Le palais de tous le Camerounais et non de qui ce soit.*
>
> Do not privatize the Etoudi (Presidential) palace,
> The palace of all Cameroonians and not that of any single personality.

The Presidential Palace at Etoudi is a national heritage and a symbol of nationhood and national pride. Thus to privatize it will be to deprive Cameroonians of a sense of belonging, purpose, and national pride.

Pillage of Natural Resources

Longue Longue also decries the fact that although Cameroon is endowed with rich and diverse natural resources which are being wantonly exploited, the majority of Cameroonians are still wallowing in abject poverty and misery. The reasons for this embarrassing situation are not hard to find. The rich and diverse natural resources which would have easily provided the capital necessary to transform the country into an emergent nation, have been plundered by the neo-colonialists with the complicity of unpatriotic Cameroonians. Even the meager funds that manage to enter state coffers are either mismanaged or embezzled. He expresses this view in "trop d'impots tuent l'impot" (2006):

> *C'est les dirigeants qui s'enrichissent mama oh eh*
> *Mais le developpement ne suit pas eh mama oh...*
> *Kilometre douze depuis vingt cinq ans, il n'y a pas d'eau*
> *Yabassi, Nkondjock, Bafang il n'y a pas de routes*

Bafia, Batouri, Yokaduma il n'y a pas d'eau
Bertoua, Ngaoundere, Kumba il n'y a pas de routes
Meme les quartiers voisins du palais oh e
Ne sont pas éclaires mama e
Meme les routes voisines du palais
Ne sont pas goudronnees mama oh

The leaders are the ones who are rolling in the lap of luxury,
But there are no worthwhile development projects in the country.
For the past twentyfive years, there is no potable water in Kilometer 12.
The roads in Yabassi, Nkondjock, Bafang are in a state of utter disrepair.
Bafia, Batouri, Yokaduma have no potable water supply.
The roads in Bertoua, Ngaoundere, Kumba are full of potholes.
Even the neighbouring quarters to the Presidential Palace
Have no electricity.
Even the roads near the Presidential Palace are not tarred.

Longue Longue in the above song cannot understand why the indigenous supporters and collaborators of the neo-colonial powers should be swimming in ostentatious and scandalous opulence while the country has no basic infrastructure as potable water, electricity and good roads. It is indeed the height of irony that while the super powers of the West have already been to the moon and back, Cameroonians are still struggling to reach their villages.

In another song, "Ayo Africa" (2001), Longue Longue reproaches the neo-colonial powers for plundering the rich and diverse natural resources of the country.

Les Blancs sont arrives chez nous.
Ils nous ont trompes et nous ont arrache nos richesses.
Nous les enfants de l'Afrique nous n'avons plus de richesses.
Regardez Bonamoussadi c'est pour les Blancs.
La foret de Yabassi toujour les Blancs.

Le petrole de l'Afrique c'est toujours les Blancs.
Le marche de bois au Congo toujour les Blancs
Thomas Sankara est mort toujours les Blancs.
La politique africaine toujour les Blancs.
La guerre civile au Zaire toujours les Blancs
Les wolowos (prostituees) en Afrique toujours les Blancs.

When the whites descended on African soil,
They deceived us and plundered our natural resources.
We, the children of Africa have been deprived of our heritage.
Look at Bonamoussadi, it is the exclusive preserve of the whites.
The forest of Yabassi is owned by the whites.
The petrol in Africa belongs to the whites.
The timber market in the Congo is reserved for the whites.
African politics are teleguided by the whites.
The civil war in Zaire is orchestrated by the whites.
African prostitutes are monopolized by the whites.

This new long-distance economic domination has not only impoverished Africans, but has also enslaved and emasculated them. As Longue Longue puts it in the same song:

Africa di work oh! Europa di chop oh
Cameroon di work French di chop oh
I say Zaire di work Belgique di chop oh
Guinea Equato di work Espagne di chop oh
Nigeria di work oh Angleterre di chop oh
Longue Longue di work Bakala di chop oh.

Africa is working but Europe is reaping the benefits oh
Cameroon is working but France is reaping the benefits oh
I say that Zaire is working but Belgium is reaping the benefits oh.
Equatorial Guinea is working but Spain is reaping the benefits oh
Nigeria is working oh but England is reaping the benefits oh

> *Longue Longue is working but the whites are reaping the benefits oh.*

Longue Longue in the above excerpt is lamenting the fact that the scandalous opulence of Europe emanates from the soil and sub-soil of Africa, and that the industrial prosperity of Europe is being built on the sweat of Africans. Mazrui (177), has also been worried by this new form of enslavement and exploitation especially when he pointed out that:

> *Africa's contribution to the West's industrialization has ranged from the era of the slave trade for Western plantations to the new era of cobalt and chrome for Western factories. The foundation of Western industrial prosperity include African labour, territory and minerals. African contribution to Western industrial development inadvertently helped to create the white technological Brahmins of the world. The West's disruptive impact on Africa helped to create the Black technological untouchables of the twentieth century.*

In the light of the above, it is obvious that the political leadership has failed to inspire or sustain popular hope in the way that they have been conducting the affairs of the nation. Hence, Cameroonians have been constrained to see themselves as pawns in a game of chess played by the political leadership.

The protest musicians as the conscience of their society, find the present state of affairs unacceptable. That is why they insist that all those who are responsible for the present state of affairs, who have perverted the country's democracy and who are thwarting all attempts at meaningful change, must pay for their devilish acts. This is the underlying theme of Lapiro's album "Na who Go Pay?" (1993):

> *S'il est vrai que la democratie en soi est une bonne chose*
> *Est que les peoples opprimes en ont besoin*
> *Afin que les minorities bouffeuses cessent*
> *De regner en maitres absolus sur les majorites affames et sans abris,*
> *Je fais aujourd'hui l'amer constat*
> *Qu'au lieu de repondre a nos problems,*
> *La democratie, detournee par de lugubres calculateurs,*

Est plutot devenue une epidemie,
Une calamite pour le petit people qui, malheureusement,
Est seule a en faire les frais

Pendant que l'organisation mondiale de la santé
Ne cesse de nous prodiguer des conseils
Pour que nous puissions nous mettre a l'abri
Des maladies susceptible de tuer beaucoup et vite,
Voila que la democratie;
Utilisee abusivement et contre tout attente
Par des vendeurs d'illusions et de mensonges,
Bat aujourd'hui tous les records de rapidite en tueries.
Mieux que le SIDA,
La mauvaise gestion de la democratie a tue beaucoup trop.

Au nom de la sainte democratie,
Les egoists et les fascists ont tout sacage.
Afin d'attiendre leurs ambitions,
Ils ont exploite le mecontentement des laisses-pour-compte.
Mecontentement du a la crise economique
Imposee a nos peoples par les bailleurs de fonds,
Avec la fixation fantaisiste du prix d'achat
De nos matieres premieres et aussi,
Mecontentement du aux mauvais partages
Des recettes de nos richesses bradees a vil prix!
Les aventuriers en ont profite
Pour faire descendre les enfants d'autrui dans les rues,
Bruler et faire tuer,
En pregnant bien sur le soin de mettre leurs progenitures,
Eux-memes, a l'abri.
Comme toujours, le petit people a ete martyrise!
Une fois de plus, les laissees-pour-compte ont servi de cobayes.

Sans le respect de l'opinion d'autrui,
Le dialogue, la tolerance, le pardon, la democratie a-t-elle sa raison d'etre?
Pourtant, nous avons besoin de la democratie: la vrai!

Celle qui nous permettra de combler le fosse des inegalites socials!
Non celle qui, mal geree, fait plus de ravages qu'une epidemie de dysenterie
Aigue!
Oui a la democratie!
Non au sacrifices des vies humaines!
Na who go pay?
Qui va payer?

If it is true that democracy in itself is a good thing
And that the oppressed people actually need it
In order to stop the kleptocratic minority from lording it
Over the famished and dispossessed majority,
Today, I make a bitter assessment
That rather than resolve our problems,
Democracy, as hijacked by subservient mediocres,
Has become an epidemic,
A calamity for the down trodden who, unfortunately,
Are the only ones condemned to pay the ultimate cost.
Just when the World Health Organisation
Is inundating us with suggestions
On how to avoid pandemics that kill several people suddenly,
There comes democracy,
Used abusively by vendors of illusions, hypocrisy and lies
Which today beats all records of sudden deaths
Even faster than the AIDS pandemic.
The perversion of democracy has prompted several sudden deaths.
In the name of Saint Democracy,
The egocentric fascists have devastated everything
In order to fulfil their selfish ambitions.
They have exploited the dissatisfaction of the wretched of the earth,
Discontent caused by the economic crisis
Imposed on our people by the international funding agencies
With the ridiculous fixing of the purchasing price
Of our natural resources.
Discontent on the uneven distribution

Of the income from our resources sold at a give away price.
The adventurers took advantage of that
To send the children of others to the streets
To destroy and thus serve as cannon fodder
While taking the precaution to send their children
And themselves to safety.
As always, it is the common people who are martyred.
Once again, the "small people" have been used as guinea pigs.

Without respect for the opinion of others,
Dialogue, tolerance, forgiveness, has democracy any justification?
Whereas, we actually need democracy: the real one!
That which will enable us to fill the lacuna of social inequalities.
Not that which has been perverted and can cause more harm
Than an epidemic of acute dysentery.
Yes to democracy!
No to wanton sacrifice of human lives!
Who will pay?
My compatriots, who will pay?

Democracy has been recognized and institutionalized as a norm by most countries as the form of government which can best protect the social contract between the governing and the governed. This is because democracy places man at the centre of the exercise of political power. It is also concerned with peace. It ensures the integrity of state institutions. It guarantees fundamental freedoms and good governance, and is more responsive to the popular concerns of the people. It also has a symbiotic relationship with economic development. But, democracy in itself is a vague concept. It has several models, and its implementation in a country is fraught with problems. Thus, there is no universal form of democracy that can be applicable everywhere in the same manner. For example, the Cameroonian Head of State, Paul Biya shares this view. That is why he designed what has come to be known as advanced democracy. That is, democracy tailored to the Cameroonian reality but based on recognized democratic paradigms. He also contends that the implementation of democracy requires a reasonable time frame because of the peculiar circumstances of the country. This is the essence of his declaration to the diplomatic corps accredited to Yaounde on 6 January, 2000 in (Agbor-Ambang and Enowfor, 2010:81-82):

> One can say today – that the western –type democracy is recognized as the regime best adapted to the conditions of the modern world. It must be said that for some ten years now, it has gained considerable ground to the detriment of essentially authoritarian regimes, notably in Africa. But common sense requires that we admit that the passage from a traditional society, characterized by respect for authority to a form of political organization based on freewill, cannot be done without a transition which takes into consideration both the mentalities of the people and the level of development.

Biya is right to say that we do not need to reinvent democracy, because there is a common bedrock on which a country can build a standard democracy. But the population must be sufficiently educated on the subject.

The protest musicians also acknowledge the need for a genuine democracy in Cameroon. But, they also contend that what is being practiced in Cameroon today is nothing short of a perverted democracy which does not guarantee power alternation and which has failed to respond to the needs of Cameroonians. In fact, the committed artists see the "counterfeit democracy" implanted in Cameroon as the principal source of political upheavals in the country as can be seen in the following lines from Lapiro's song cited above:

> Without respect for the opinion of others.
> Dialogue, tolerance, forgiveness, has democracy any raison d'etre?
> Whereas we actually need democracy : the real one!
> That which will enable us to fill the gaps of social inequalities.
> Not that which has been wrongly managed and can cause more harm
> Than an epidemic of acute dysentery.

> *Yes to democracy!*
> *No to sacrifices of human life!*

Lapiro is saying that the perverted democracy inherited from the West was again doctored by the Cameroonian political leadership to suit their selfish interests. Consequently, it cannot possibly meet the aspirations of the people. Hence the need for a true democracy. But, the question remains, what kind of democracy can thrive in the face of such pervasive corruption?

Having noted the intense sense of disillusionment and of betrayal among the down trodden Cameroonians the protest musicians decide to speak out rather than gnash their teeth in silence. Hence they do no mince their words. They blame the Cameroonians themselves for being the architects of their own mass misery. This is reminiscent of Achebe's often quoted proverb that "the man who brings ant-infested faggots into his hut should not grumble when lizards begin to pay him visits."

Therefore, by calling on Cameroonians to take their destiny into their own hands, the protest musicians are saying two things. Firstly, that marginality, though a real handicap, can also help to unleash collective energies for change and transformation. Secondly, that Cameroonians themselves must be ready to fight their own fight. But, one question which the musician have failed to address is, how long the situation is likely to last? Nyamnjoh (118) however proposes an answer:

> *But as the national cake diminishes with the worsening economic crisis, corruption, mass misery and ethnicity, it becomes more illusive for the bulk of small people to claim the same or any benefits from their connections with the big – or the not so big – men and women in power. The crumbling of lucrative networks of patronage and influence that have linked the masses and the elite, championed national politics and frustrated most attempts at bringing about a more democratic dispensation over the years, could well be the beginning of a long awaited revolution. And the ruling elite might well have reason soon to exclaim: "les choses qui arrivent aux autres commence déjà a m'arriver!*

CHAPTER FIVE
THE WAY FORWARD

> *The feeling is growing, even among pessimistic scholars, that however entrenched, tyranny in Cameroon today is a candle in the wind. Its days, it is hoped are numbered, thanks to mounting disillusionment, international pressure, and the growing recognition by the masses of the importance of organized resistance to government repression (Nyamnjoh).*

In the previous chapter, I demonstrated how the protest musicians have tried to deconstruct the programmes of the post-colonial and neo-colonial power structures. But, if the protest artists stopped at deconstruction alone, they would have carried out an exercise in futility; for we deconstruct in order to reconstruct. Therefore, this chapter is devoted to reconstruction. That is, it will examine what the protest musicians see as the way forward for Cameroon and what they propose as strategies to get the country out of the difficult and embarrassing political and economic situation in which it is mired. Nyamnjoh (115) summarizes the moribund situation thus:

> *Since the advent of the new wave of multipartism in 1991: Cameroonians have had little reason to believe that they are anything other than pawns in a game of chess played by the power elite; the latter set their agenda for them, use them to serve their ends, and at the end of the day, abandon them to the misery and ignorance to which they have been accustomed. Democracy is yet to become a way of life – a culture – in Cameroon; so far it has served mainly as a face powder, an empty concept or slogan devoid of concrete meaning used to justify reactionary propaganda by the CPDM and its acolytes, on the one hand, and revolutionary propaganda by the opposition and some pressure groups, on the other.*

As a consequence of the Cameroonian predicament which Nyamnjoh has described most succinctly above, there is a consensus of opinion among Cameroonians that things have degenerated to such an extent that there is no way that the impasse can be resolved politically. The reasons for this are not hard to find. The one party structure in the country was transformed into a hegemonic party system in the early 1990s. The incumbent dominant CPDM party naturally encouraged the creation of several opposition parties on the tenuous grounds that the democratization process does not impose any limits to the number of political parties that can be created in a country. The result is that Cameroon now has well over 230 legalized political parties for a population of about 20 million. This is a clear indication of political immaturity. These peripheral, opportunistic factions, which go under the name of political parties, crystallized on family, ethnic, and regional lines with the aims of supporting the centre party and gathering the spoils from political fallouts. To complicate matters, the dominant CPDM party transformed some of these subordinate factions into satellite parties under the pseudonym of "Presidential Majority" ostensibly to justify the existence of genuine democracy in Cameroon. But in reality, to circumnavigate the possibility of any power-alternation in the country.

    The protest musicians who have taken stock of the debilitating situation, arrived at the conclusion that the bulk of Cameroonians hanker after a change for the better. But they also realize that under the hegemonic party system, neither the incumbent dominant CPDM party nor the personalized, semi-loyal, micro parties can provide workable solutions to the current disillusionment. Even the so-called credible, openly disloyal opposition parties like the SDF, UPC, and CDU cannot guarantee the institutionalization of freedom and democracy in the country. As Nyamnjoh (114) has reiterated:

> *Faced with many grievances and demands from poor social groups, the supply of ideas from political leaders has remained limited. It seems as though the general concern of the opposition parties is to substitute the ruling bellies, and not the well-being of everyone.*

> *Again, the quarrel of the opposition is, more with the eaters than with the eating.... Denunciations of malpractice in high office, by the opposition, appear more and more as mere political gimmicks, as even the most radical of them have not sought to go beyond what Monga has termed slogans in line with populist illusion.*

The direct consequence of the above statement is that the opposition in Cameroon is so fragmented that the political system is virtually left with the incumbent dominant party. Thus, it becomes difficult for one to see any real difference between the opposition and the dominant political party in power. In the absence of a credible opposition and a vigorous civil society therefore, the protest musicians perceive themselves as the only pro-democracy agency capable of countering the activities of undemocratic forces and fighting for genuine democracy and the empowerment and edification of ostracized Cameroonians. Their position is strengthened by the fact that they have vision and, since they live and have their being in the society, it follows logically that they have a clear conception of their society and, consequently, the way they want the society to go. That is why Dit Combat in his song, "You Cannot Lie Forever" (2003) can tell the people in power that he has seen through the ideological pretences which they use as ploy to deceive the suffering masses:

> *You cannot lie to me forever no, no.*
> *You cannot fool me forever.*
> *Whatever you show*
> *On your worldwide display,*
> *Whatever we see,*
> *We know what games you play.*
> *No one can stop time,*
> *No one can change our mind.*
>
> *Whatever story you make up to explain,*
> *Whatever money you give to ease our pain,*
> *You cannot fool me forever.*
> *And no money can buy us,*
> *Whether dollars or euros*
> *Because we are no longer on sale.*
> *Because we have learnt from history,*

> *Two hundred years of slavery*
> *That is why you can no longer deceive us.*

The gist of Dit Combat's song is that the political leadership might have succeeded in deceiving Cameroonians with hypocrisy and lies in the past but that is no longer possible because disaffected Cameroonians in their numbers are becoming politically aware. They are seeing through all the mystifications used by the corrupt leaders to consolidate their hold on power. The people now want a change for the better. They also want to have an active say in all matters of public interest. Finally, they are counting on the protest musicians as critics and social commentators to educate them and to help them to reclaim their stolen freedom.

Longue Longue, the self-styled advocate of the ostracized masses continues the criticism of the people in power from where Dit Combat stopped. He accuses the political leaders who have taken the oath of office for betraying the aspirations of the people without compunction:

> *C'est vous, c'est vous*
> *C'est vous qui avez prête serment oh*
> *Devant Dieu et les homes oh*
> *Que vous allez bien travailler eh eh*
> *Je m'addresse aux assermentes: docteurs, magistrats,*
> *Collecteurs d'empots, douaniers, elus du people ecouter*
> *C'est vous que avez prete serment devant Dieu et les homes*
> *Que le pays va changer eh eh*
> *Alors que rien n'a changer.*
>
> *La population wuna tok*
> *C'est vous, c'est vous qui avez prete serment*
> *Que le pays va changer*
> *C'est vous, c'est vous que avez prete serment*
> *Qu'il y aura du boulot pour tout le monde*
> *C'est vous, c'est vous que avez prete serment*
> *Time di go mandat de bole oh oh*
> *Rien ne bouge, le pays ne fait que s'enfoncer...*
> *Les riches ne font que s'enricher*
> *Les pauvres ne font que s'appauvrir*

Les plus faibles meurent du paludisme
Ou est donc l'avenir de ce pays?
Les pauvres ne font que s'appauvrir
Les plus faibles meurent du cholera
Ou est donc l'avenir de l'Afrique?

Population wuna tok
C'est vous c'est vous mah
C'est vous que avez prete serment
Qu'il aura du boulot pour tout le monde
Pourtant nous payons nos impots mama oh
Pourtant nous payons nos impots mama oh
Et le developpement ne suit pas mama oh
Et le developpement ne suit pas mama oh
C,est le collecteur d'impots qui s'enrichir mama oh
C'est le dirigeant qui s'enrichir mama oh.

You are those who took the oath of office.
You are those who took the oath of office before God and man
That you will work well.
I am addressing the experts sworn on oath: doctors, magistrates, revenue collectors, custom officers, parliamentarians
Listen!
You are those who took the oath to change the country,
But nothing has changed.
Compatriots, speak up!
You are those, you are those who took the oath of office
That there will be employment for all.
You are those, you are those who took the oath of office
Days are going by, terms of office are ending
Nothing moves, the country is only sliding into recession.
The rich are getting richer,
While the poor are getting poorer.
The very weak are dying of malaria
Where then is the future of this country?
The rich are getting richer,
While the poor are getting poorer.
The very weak are dying of cholera.
Where then is the future of Africa?

> *Compatriots, speak up!*
> *You are those, you are those mah*
> *You are those who took the oath of office*
> *That there will be employment for all*
> *And yet we pay our taxes mama oh*
> *And yet we pay our taxes mama oh*
> *And yet we pay our taxes mama oh*
> *But development is not following mama oh*
> *But development is not following mama oh*
> *It is the revenue collector who gets richer*
> *It is the power elite that get richer.*

Longue Longue is incensed by the fact that the idealistic rhetoric of the political elite generated expectations of a better life in many Cameroonians. Unfortunately, these expectations were never fulfilled. A privileged minority continue to enjoy an ostentatious life style which separates them from the vast majority of the population still groveling in misery. Thus, the artist sees the power elite's commitment to improving the general welfare of the masses as a hypocritical cover for maintaining the status quo. Afo Akom is also fed up with the ideological pretences, hypocrisy and lies of the ruling elite. That is why he fulminates against the empty rhetoric of the system in the following lines culled from his album "Dong Ibodem":

> *Le chemin du success n'est pas du tout facile come pensait L'homme paresseux.*
> *Apres mon constat, la voiture a ete fabriquee pour suivre la route*
> *Et non la route pour suivre la voiture…*
> *On dit suivent que les enfants d'aujourd'hui sont les grands de demain*
> *Mais quand je regarde a gauche, je regarde a droit,*
> *On se dit ou est l'avenir de ces enfants?*
> *Pendant que les autres sont la pour lutter pour l'avenir de ces enfants*
> *Avec les grandes ambitions*
> *Les autres sont la pour lutter pour leur ventre.*

> *The road to success is not as easy as the lazy man thinks.*
> *From my assessment of the situation, a vehicle is manufactured to follow the road*
> *And not the road to follow the vehicle.*
> *It is often said that the children of today are the leaders of tomorrow.*
> *But when I look to the left and to the right,*
> *One wonders where the future of these children lie?*
> *While others are fighting to build a bright future for these children*
> *With great ambition*
> *Others are there only to fight for their bellies.*

The last line of the above excerpt, "others are there only to fight for their bellies" refers to the extravagant greed of those in high office. Afo Akom denounces the over-riding ambition of these unpatriotic Cameroonians which, put quite simply, is to plunder the country. For them, life is entirely a material affair. No effort should therefore be spared in the pursuit of such material madness. The enraged musician continues his fustigation with biting sarcasm:

> *Les musiciens on chante qu'on ne change jamais une equipe qui gagne.*
> *Mais la question que je me pose:*
> *Est-ce que en Afrique on peut facilement changer une equipe qui gagne?*
> *Meme si cette equipe gagne avec la complicite de l'arbitre de touché*
> *Et des entrants sans oblier le commissaire du match...*
> *After a long struggle when success don begin come*
> *Lazy people dem go say you don take na mammy water...*
> *When some are fighting for the future*
> *Others are fighting for their bellies*
>
> *Musicians have sung that one never changes a winning team*
> *But, the question that I ask is,*
> *Is it easy to change a winning team in Africa?*
> *Even if the team wins with the complicity of the lines men*

> *And the entrants not forgetting the match commissioner? ...*
> *After a long struggle when success is in sight*
> *Lazy people will say that you have used magic ...*
> *While some are fighting for the future*
> *Others are fighting for their bellies.*

Afo Akom's use of the analogy of the football match is interesting. He sees the game of political power like a football match in which you need to prepare the players physically and psychologically if the intention is to win. Both football and politics have clear cut ground rules. Both games require competitive and team spirit, fair play and a level playing ground. But, both games also have their seamy sides. Football provides the possibility of consulting a sorcerer, corrupting the referee and the lines men, or even bribing your opponents and other match officials to bend the rules in your favour. Politics, on the other hand, also gives room for bribery, the use of occultism and, in extreme cases, physical assault and battery on opponents and intimidation of the electorate.

Attitude to Change

The ruling elite, the marginalized people and the protest musicians all agree that the state of affairs in the country is so deplorable that it calls for immediate and radical change. The problem however is that change means different things to these groups of Cameroonians. Generally speaking, change means the way one thing can become another. If the thing is transformed by a gradual process, it is called growth or evolution. If, on the other hand, the change is violent or disruptive, it is called a revolution. Change can also be from within or from without. Some people welcome change. Others are suspicious of change. Yet others prefer to maintain the status quo. As Robert Green (2000:396) points out,

> *Human psychology contains many dualities one of them being that even while people understand the need for change, knowing how important it is for institutions and individuals to be occasionally renewed, they are also irritated and upset by changes that affect them*

personally. They know that change is necessary, and that novelty provides relief from boredom, but deep inside they cling to the past. Change in the abstract, or superficial change, they desire, but a change that upset core habits and routines is deeply disturbing to them. Those who find themselves in positions of power, see those positions as their birthright. Consequently, they see change as something that can help them to remain in power permanently. Those who find themselves in the opposition parties and who are seeking to take over power see change as a means of substituting the "ruling bellies" rather than as a means of seeking the wellbeing of everyone. That is why they seek revolutionary change. To the by-passed people, change means the recognition of their human worth and value. Thus, it is intended to generate greater freedom and to improve their welfare. Seen in this light, change is expected to expand and empower.

With the need for change established, the next question is, what kind of change can the masses accommodate? Nyamnjoh (118) attempts an answer:

Cameroonians are, as a result, a very patient people. And whoever calls for a change of system before everyone or every group has had their own turn or 'fair' share at the high table ('la mangeoire'), is unlikely to command much support. Especially as thanks to the system, Cameroonians judge one another not so much by the merits of what they say or do, but rather by the stereotypes and prejudices for which their ethnic group or region are known. Anyone who speaks up in favour of democratic change quickly gets labeled as a self-seeking 'utopist' or 'marchand d'illusions' and accused accordingly of trying to use 'innocent Cameroonians' as a stepping stone for selfish and ethnic ambitions.

In Nyamnjoh's opinion, Cameroonians are allergic to too much innovation. As a result, whatever change is envisaged, must be slow and administered in small doses. Here then lies the reason for the failure of the revolutionary approach adopted by the Cameroonian opposition parties to the democratization process. It is common knowledge that whenever election irregularities are alleged in the country, the opposition parties are quick to incite the innocent masses to take to the streets in protest. In most cases, these protests and demonstrations degenerate into violence with heavy loss of human lives. Ironically, these political upheavals always leave the incumbent leader firmly in control. That explains why the protest musicians avoid the bellicose approach to change and instead espouse peaceful protests and the gradualist approach.

The sinister and intimidating moves by the ruling elite to retain their hold on power, have made nonsense of the whole concept of change. This is the gist of the following satirical song by Longue Longue:

> Vous nous avez promis le changement
> On attend donc ce changement
> Vous allez meme changer quoi?
> L'argent des impots que vous ne faites que detourner
> Avec la vie que vous ne faites que nous compliquer
> Changement, on attend le changement
> J. Remy Ngono veut le changement
> Aujourd'hui meme a Nkoulouloun les sauveteurs ne font que pleurer
> Que c'est dur.
> I say if you go for Bamenda oh, bayam sellam dem di cry eh
> Dem say I di strong eh
>
> Ou est donc le changement?
> On attend, on attend, on attend le changement.
> Vous allez meme changer quoi?
> La constitution ou les eternel ministres?
> Vous nous avez promis le changement
> On attend donc ce changement oh!
> Vous allez meme changer quoi?
> Avec les impots que vous ne faites que augmenter
> Avec la vie que vous ne faites que nous compliquer
> Changement, on attend le changement
> Il faute changer oh!
> Longue Longue, le sacrifie du people.
>
> You promised us change we are therefore waiting for it.
> What are you even going to change?
> You only embezzle our tax money

While complicating our lives.
Change, we are waiting for the change
J. Remy Ngono wants change.
If you go to Nkoulouloun today, hawkers are only crying of hardship...
I repeat, if you go to Bamenda oh, petty traders are only crying that things are difficult.
Where then is the change?
We are waiting, we are waiting, we are waiting for the change
What are you even going to change?
The constitution or your "sit tight" ministers?
You promised us change,
We are waiting for the change
What are you even going to change?
With the taxes that you keep increasing,
With life which you keep complicating.

Change, we are waiting for the change!
Longue Longue, the sacrificed of the people.

The word "change" has been used in this passage ten times to draw attention to the fact that that is what the people really need but that is not what the politicians are giving them. Thus sustainable change if it is to come at all, it must come from the people themselves. That is exactly what the musicians are telling their people. But, change in Cameroon will come to nothing unless governance is improved and governance cannot be improved unless the oppressed people themselves undertake to improve it. This is where the crucial role of the protest songs becomes apparent. There is no doubt that if the songs are properly appreciated and understood, they can help to raise the level of consciousness of the marginalized masses and, in so doing, catalyze positive change in the country.

    The protest musicians have proposed several strategies for getting their beleaguered country out of the parlous straits in which it is entangled. But, for the purposes of this chapter, I will limit myself only to those schemes which I consider to be germane. These include introspection, promoting the work ethic, empowering rural women, and flagellating Cameroon's morally bankrupt leaders.

Introspection

The protest musicians are disturbed by the fact that members of the ruling class are either unwilling or unable to rise to the challenge of living by precepts. They do not demonstrate any sense of individual or collective responsibility. In short, they have deliberately swept aside the morality of good governance. That is why Longue Longue in the following song, exhorts them to examine their conscience:

>On ne cache pas la lumiere du soleil Longue Longue, le liberateur libere
>Avant de te moquer de moi, il faut te regarder eh
>Dans un miroir oh oh il faut te regarders oh.
>Avant de juger les autres il faut te critique eh
>Dans un miroir oh oh, il faut te regarder eh.
>
>Que celui qui me tue ne reste pas mourir.
>Avant de te moquer de moi il faut te regarder eh
>Dans un miroir il faut te regarder eh
>Avant de parler oh oh il faut reflechir
>Dans un miroir il faut te regarder eh
>Avant de me culpabiliser il faut reflechir eh
>Dans un miroir, il faut te regarder.
>
>*Sunlight cannot be hidden, Longue Longue, the liberator liberated.*
>*Before you mock at me, you should take a look at yourself eh*
>*In a mirror, you should take a look at yourself.*
>*Before you judge others, you should carry out an autocritique*
>*In a mirror, you should take a look at yourself.*
>*Let the person who is killing me not die later.*
>
>*Before you mock at me, you should look at yourself*
>*In a mirror you should take a good look at yourself.*
>*Before you judge others, you should carry out an autocritique.*
>*In a mirror, you should take a good look at yourself.*
>*Before you speak you should pause and reflect*
>*You should take a look at yourself in a mirror.*

You should think twice before you condemn me.
In a mirror, you should take a good look at yourself.

Longue Longue is, in effect, calling on the corrupt and inept political leaders who have come to see governance as a matter of how long they are able to cling to power, to undertake an exercise in soul searching before acting. Three wise sayings readily come to mind here. The first is, "it is when people are drunk that they lose all inhibitions and reveal their true selves". The second is," judge not that you be not judged". And the third is, "when you dig a hole of wickedness, make it shallow for you may be the one to fall into it". Longue Longue then goes on to highlight the principles of the law of karma in order to emphasize the political nemesis that awaits them if they continue on their downward trend towards perdition.

Avant de condamner, faites un examen de conscience
Car chacun sera juge
Vous qui torturer le people, faites attention
Ce people vous jugera
Dieu vous regarde, on vous connait déjà
Les critiques seront critiques
Toi qui condamne oh oh oh
Un jour tu sera condamne oh oh
Toi que juges eh eh
Un jour tu seras juge oh oh...
Toi qui condamnes oh oh Mr. President eh
Chacun a son tour chez le coiffeur
Vous avez libere le coupable envoye l'innocent en prison
Le pauvre innocent a la tole
Vous m'avez condamne sans que je ne sois juge
Dieu vous regarde, on vous connait déjà...
Tu dis bas la corruption pourtant tu es corrumpu

Tu dis bas les corrumpu pourtant tu es corrupteur
Tu dis a bas l'escroquerie pourtant tu es receleur eh eh eh
Ah oui Longue Longue, j'en ai marre!
Marre de l'injustice, marre de la trahison, mare du chantage!
Quand vous mangez les populations ont faim, c'est la guerre

Toi qui croyais que tu es déjà arrive
Toi qui croyais que tu es déjà arrive
Toi qui croyais que tu es au dessus de la loi...
Aujourd'hui les choses ont change oh oh Lomba eh
Aujourd'hui le pouvoir est tombe eh eh
Toi qui detournais les fonds publics
Aujourd'hui on va te condemner eh eh
Bamenda I go tok oh...

Before you pass judgement, examine your conscience
Because everyone will be judged.
You who torture people, be careful,
The people will judge you.
God sees you. We know you already.

The critics will be criticized.
You who pass judgement eh eh eh
One day you will also be sentenced oh oh oh
You who judge others, eh eh
One day you will also be judged oh oh

You have freed the guilty and imprisoned the innocent.
You shower praises on the big thieves and sentence the small thieves.
You who judge eh eh eh
One day you will also be judged
You who pass judgement oh oh Mr. President eh
Everyone in his own turn at the barber's.
You have freed the guilty and imprisoned the innocent.
The innocent poor to the gallows.

You sentenced me without trial
God sees you. We know you already.

You say down with corruption whereas you are the corrupt.
You say down with the corrupt whereas you are corrupter.
You say down with crookery whereas you are the receiver.
Ah yes Longue Longue, I am angry!

Angry at the injustice, angry at the betrayal, angry at the chicanery!
When you are satiating yourself, the population is dying of hunger.
It is war!
You who think that you have arrived,
You who think that you are above the law
Today things have changed oh oh Lomba oh.
Today power has collapsed eh eh.
You who embezzle public funds,
Today you will be sentenced.
Bamenda I will speak.

This song is somehow prophetic. Angered by the debilitating and crippling corruption in the country, incensed by the fact that those in positions of power and responsibility are living in scandalous luxury and opulence in a country where half the population is living below the breadline, and hearkening to the pleas of millions of dispossessed Cameroonians, the President of the Republic was obliged to establish the dreaded "operation Sparrow Hawk" which is creating a wave of panic among the ruling elite, and which has already occasioned the arrests and sentencing of several Government ministers and senior administrators to long terms of imprisonment for embezzlement and misuse of public funds. Thus, in Cameroon today, the "high and mighty" who once thought that they were above the law, are languishing in jail. This is another indication that the cries of the protest musicians are being heard by the powers that be.

Promoting the Work Ethic

In the Cameroon civil service, laissez faire prevails. Punctuality, assiduity, effective presence at work, accountability, respect of hierarchy, and discipline are anathema. Government property lacks sanctity and can be abused and misappropriated without qualms. Senior civil servants are too spineless to resist the temptations of the corrupting influence of both privilege and positions of power. They therefore collude with corrupt political officials and gradually succumb to the temptations of unbridled materialism. With time, they begin to resemble the corrupt politicians. Since Cameroonians in general regard life as an entirely material affair, covetousness has become a way of life and greed the driving force behind most actions. Hard work has naturally been forced to take the back seat while youths are brought up to shun manual work. That is why they flock to the urban centres in search of white collar jobs. Andre Marie Tala understands the implications of this negative philosophy and admonishes Cameroonians to avoid such unbridled pursuit for wealth and adopt the work ethic and a sense of civic responsibility. In his song "crise" (1989), he calls on his fellow Cameroonians to shun indolence and laxity, and embrace hard work.

> *Voici venu le temps de la disette*
> *Reveille-toi! Reveille-toi!*
> *Pourquoi gardes-tu encore le lit?*
> *Leve-toi avant l'aurore*
> *Pourquoi gardes-tu encore le lit?*
> *Reveille-toi avant les oiseaux.*
> *En temps de crise, l'une des solutions: le travail!*
> *En temps de crise, l'une des solutions: la rigueur!*
> *En temps de crise, l'une des solutions: l'integration!*
> *En temps de crise, l'une des solutions: l'imagination! ...*
> *Voici venu le mauvais temps;*
> *Gardons- nous des comportements negatives*
> *De peur qu'il ne nous manqué jusq'a l'eau a boire?*
> *Voice venu le temps de la disette,*
> *Gardons-nous des comportements negatives*
> *De peur que la famine ne gagne tout le terrain? ...*
> *En temps de crise, l'une des solutions: moins de gachis*
> *En temps de crise, l'une des solutions: plus de volunte*
> *En temps de crise, il faut travailler*
> *En temps de crise, travailler plus.*
>
> *Here comes inauspicious times,*
> *Wake up! Wake up!*
> *Why are you still lying in bed?*
>
> *Get up before dawn.*

> *Why are you still lying in bed?*
> *Get up before the birds.*
> *In times of crisis, one of the solutions: work!*
> *In times of crisis, one of the solutions: rigour!*
> *In times of crisis, one of the solutions: integration!*
> *In times of crisis, one of the solutions: imagination! ...*
> *Here comes inauspicious times,*
> *Should we maintain our negative attitudes*
> *For fear that we may lack even water to drink?*
> *Here comes the period of famine,*
> *Should we maintain our negative attitudes*
> *For fear that famine will engulf us all? ...*
> *In times of crisis, one of the solutions: less waste!*
> *In times of crisis, one of the solutions: more will power!*
> *In times of crisis, you have to work!*
> *In times of crisis, work harder!*

Tala's call is salutary because Cameroon's underdevelopment is attributable in part to the gross disregard of the work ethic by Cameroonians. But, Tala is not only concerned with the civil servants. He also extends his concern to farmers who have the arduous task of feeding the nation. He encourages them not to be discouraged by the difficulties that they encounter in tilling the land:

> *Ne nous faisons pas trop de soucis*
> *Sur les efforts que nous imposent*
> *Nos different travaux*
> *Car nous n'en serons que fort recompenses.*
>
> *Travail, c'est peiner*
> *Mais qu'y pouvons-nous?*
> *Un proverb de chez nous dit avec justesse*
> *Que 'le travail d'aujourd'hui,*
> *Est la richesse de demain".*
>
> *Maman vous le recommande:*
>
> *Faites un tour demain au champ*
> *Sourtout, ne manqué pas d'y aller*
> *Nos champs sont remplis de succulents champignons*
> *Que vous ne manques pas de ramassez*
> *Dans une delicieuse sauce jaune*

Vous serez aux anges!

Sur le chemin des plantations
Les ronces vous meutrissent le visage:
Mais une fois rentres a la maison,
Vous oblierez toutes ces peines
Au moment de savoure vos recoltes.

Il vous arrive de vous etonner face a certain success
Et vous dites: "quelle reussite!"
Cette reussite la n'est que la prix de l'effort.
Lorsque l'on vous presente de belle ignames,
Vous les trouvez belle en effet.
Lorque l'on vous presente de gros epis de mais
Vous vous exclamez: "quells beaux epis?"
Ne nous y trompons point
Toutes ces bonnes recoltes s'expliquent
Pas la piene qu'on 'est donnee pour les produire.

We should not worry too much
Over the efforts that we put into whatever we do
Because we will be compensated in the long run.
To work is to struggle, but what can we do?
As a local proverb puts it,
"The labour of today
Is the riches of tomorrow".

Mother has advised
Make a round of the farms.
Do not fail to do so

For our farms are full of succulent mushrooms
Which you should not fail to pick up in a bowl of
delicious yellow sauce.
You will be with the angels!

On the way to the plantations
Brambles will bruise your face,
But once you are back home,
You will forget all the pains
At the time you are appreciating your harvest.

You may even wonder at your success,
And exclaim, what success?
That success is the fruit of your efforts!

When you are presented with healthy yam tubers,
You appreciate them.
When you are presented with healthy corn cobs,
You exclaim, what beautiful cobs!
Do not be deceived.
All the bumper harvests are explained
By the labour you put into producing them.

Tala is saying here that agriculture is a noble but demanding profession, and that all those who engage in it and persevere are usually rewarded with bountiful harvests. This message is also addressed to the youths who have been afflicted with the 419 mentality and the get -rich-quick syndrome. The underlying message here is that the inordinate pursuit of wealth using uncanny underhand tactics usually leads to self-distruction. The point must however be made that Tala does not discourage the pursuit of wealth. His concern is with the methods of achieving such goals. The crucial point here, then, is that Cameroonians, especially the youths should always look beyond the pursuit of perverted values.

Empowering Rural Women
The most striking characteristic of the life style of Cameroon is that it is predominantly rural and agricultural. This is because the country is blessed with vast fertile and arable land. Thus, Cameroon has the potential of feeding not only itself but the entire central African sub-region. Yet, it is ironical that Cameroon imports almost half of the food it consumes. The reasons for this unacceptable situation are that the agricultural sector is not mechanized and the rural women who are the backbone of the country's food production are not empowered. In fact, they are neither consulted nor involved in discussions concerning food production in the country. Thus, Afo Akom is rendering an invaluable service to the rural women by being their mouthpiece and by bringing their plight to public

attention. This is the gist of his album "Femme Rurale" (2000):

> Si quelque chose a ete faite,
> Pour ameliorer la situation de la femme rurale
> Beaucoup reste a faire.
> A la premiere dame de notre pays
> Et a toutes les dames du monde,
> La femme rurale compte sur vous.
>
> Femme rurale oh oh travaillon la terre
> Femme rurale nourissons le monde
> Femme rurale oh oh travaillon la terre
> Femme rurale nourisson le monde.
>
> La mission de notre pays
> C'est de consolider sa securite alimentaire
> Sur l'etendu du territoire national oh oh
> Le developpement de notre pays tout entire en depend.
> Modernizer et diversifier notre agriculture,
> Notre elevage et pisciculture.
> ...
> Jeunesse Camerounaise et africaine,
> N'hesitez pas a retourner a la terre
> Car l'agriculture est un métier noble,
> Prêt a vous accueiller.
> De Ngaoundere a Garoua, a Maroua au Cameroun,
> De Kano a Lagos a Abuja au Nigeria
> De Kenya a Bamako
> A Dakar au Senegal
> Travaillon la terre.
>
> MINAGRI tell wuna say, FAO tell wuna say,
> WFP tell wuna say
> We must work the land and feed the world.
> ...
> At the time weh rural women de cry for salvation,
> For lack of farm to market roads to guarantee food security
> A timely intervention from our First Ladies
> Is a matter of urgency.

*Fellow country men, Sango and Nyango, agriculture is
a noble profession.
A food programme supported by our Ministry of
Agriculture
Will be of great help to us.
We must continue to modernize and diversify our
agriculture,
Stock breeding, pig farming and pisciculture
Which goes to create more jobs.
According to His Excellency the Head of State,
Poverty which is the inability to satisfy one's needs,
Will be completely eradicated.
La creativite ne se vent pas au marche
Creativity is not sold in the market.*

*If something has been done
To ameliorate the condition of the rural woman,
Much still remains to be done.
To the First Lady of our country,
And to all the First Ladies of the world,
The rural woman counts on you.*

*Rural women oh oh cultivate the land
Rural women feed the world.
Rural women oh oh cultivate the land
Rural women feed the world.*

*The mission of our country
Is to consolidate our food self-sufficency
Throughout the national territory.
Since the development of our entire nation depends on
it.
Modernize and diversify our agriculture,
Our stock breeding and pisciculture.*

*Young Cameroonians and Africans
Do not hesitate to return to the land
Because agriculture is a noble profession
Ready to receive you.
From Ngaoundere, to Garoua, to Maroua in Cameroon,
From Kano to Lagos to Abuja in Nigeria,
From Kenya to Bamako*

> *To Dakar in Senegal,*
> *Cultivate the land.*
> *MINAGRI tells you that, FAO tells you that,*
> *WFP tells you that*
> *We must cultivate the land and feed the world.*
> *...*
> *At the time when rural women are crying for salvation,*
> *For farm to market roads to guarantee food self-sufficiency,*
> *A timely intervention from our First Ladies*
> *Is a matter of urgency.*
>
> *Fellow countrymen, Sango and Nyango, agriculture is a noble profession.*
> *A food programme supported by our Ministry of Agriculture*
> *Will be of great assistance to us.*
>
> *We must continue to modernize and diversify our agriculture,*
> *Stock breeding and pisciculture*
> *Which help to create more jobs.*
> *According to His Excellency, the Head of State,*
>
> *Poverty which is the inability to satisfy one's needs*
> *Will be completely eradicated.*
> *Creativity is not sold in the market (x2).*

Afo Akom in the above song acts as the spokesperson of the rural woman. While acknowledging the fact that she must work very hard if she is to achieve the goal of feeding the nation, he notes that she needs the full support and assistance of the government and the international agencies dealing with food production.

He acknowledges the fact that the Cameroon government is working towards increasing food production in the country. But he also notes that the government could do much more. He goes on to state that instead of concentrating development projects in the urban areas as is the case at present, some of the projects could be taken to the rural areas. Such a move will help to stem the rural urban exodus. It will lead to an increase in food production thereby ensuring food self-sufficiency. It will empower the rural woman and, it will give agriculture the place it deserves in the country's development programme. The artist also calls on the government to recognize the rural women, train them, motivate them and ameliorate their living and working conditions through financial assistance, training programmes, improved health care, improved farm to market roads, providing improved seedlings, and modernizing and diversifying the agricultural sector. Finally, he solicits the help of the Cameroonian and other African First Ladies perhaps because the best advocate of the woman is the woman.

Nationhood and National Integration
I have made the point in a previous chapter that because of their chequered history, the new form of governance, and the imperial (mis) representation of Cameroon and its peoples and cultures , Cameroonians do not have a sense of belonging and purpose fifty years after the attainment of political independence. The loyalty of a Cameroonian remains more to his ethnic or tribal group than to an amorphous concept called the Cameroonian nation. Another reason is that those who inherited power at independence did not have a sense of responsibility; they were not patriotic and they did not have the ability to meet the new challenges and specificities of their new nation. They entered politics not because they were intent on serving their people, but, specifically because of its lure, and the prestige and power it gave them. Their entry into politics also seemed to have destroyed any morality that they might have had thereby transforming them into self-seeking and unscrupulous activists. Hence, their official rhetoric revolved around the creation of a unified nation capable of achieving its historic destiny. But, in practice, those in power worked, and are still working towards national deconstruction. In other words, the idea of national unity and national integration are being used as a smokescreen to camouflage the glaring disparity between the idealism of the official rhetoric and the

stark reality on the ground. That explains why the radical protest musicians are particularly disgusted with the hypocrisy of the nation building rhetoric, and why they use their songs to raise the consciousness of the people so that they can wake up to the deceit and work resolutely towards real unity and peaceful co-existence. This is the central message that Tala conveys in his album "Vivre Ensemble":

> *Ce message est dedie a la nouvelle generation africaine.*
> *Je n'ai pas choisi de naitre au Sud.*
> *Tu n'as pas choisi de naitre a l'Est,*
> *Il n'a pas choisi de naitre au Nord*
> *Je n'ai pas choisi de naitre a l'Ouest.*
> *Nous sommes condamnes a vivre ensemble.*
> *Luttons coude a coude pou notre survie;*
> *Oeuvrons dans l'amour pour notre devenir.*
> *Nos querelles intestines nuisent a nos ardeus.*
> *Notre division aide l'ennemi.*
> *Le monde se regroupe dans un village*
> *Nourrissons cette richesse qu'est l'unite*
> *Unisons nos efforts, la victoire n'est pas loin*
> *Tout acte aujourd'hui conditionne l'avenir.*
>
> *Conjuguons nos idees pour batir ce relais*
> *Que servira de pont pour nos enfants*
> *Que sont condamnes a vivre ensemble*
> *La nation interpelle chacun de ses fils*
> *Homes de sciences, paysans,*
> *Fonctionnaires et commercants*
>
> *Un effort sutenu attend chacun de nous*
> *Ainsi nous seron prets pour le troisieme millenaire.*
>
> *This message is dedicated to the new generation of Africans*
>
> *I did not choose to be born in the South.*
> *You did not choose to be born in the East.*
> *He did not choose to be born in the North*
> *I did not choose to be born in the West.*
> *We are condemned to live together*
> *Let us fight elbow to elbow for our survival,*

> *Let us work in love for our future.*
> *Our intestinal quarrels are detrimental to our enthusiasm.*
> *Our division works in favour of our enemy.*
> *The world is regrouping into a village*
> *We should nourish this wealth which is unity.*
> *We should join forces, victory is near.*
> *Our actions today will determine our future.*
> *We should unite our ideas to build the link*
> *Which will serve as a bridge for our children*
> *Who are condemned to live together.*
> *The nation is calling on all her sons*
> *Scientists, peasants, civil servants and traders*
> *A sustained effort awaits each of us*
> *and so we will be ready for theThird Millennium.*

This song is predicated on the adage "united we stand, divided we fall". The artist strongly feels that the generation of Cameroonians who were granted political independence have failed woefully to unite the various ethnic groups to create a strong sense of unity and national identity. That is why he is addressing himself to the younger generation whom he sees as the only hope for a united Cameroon. Another socially engaged artist who believes in the adage "Unity is Strength" is Afo Akom, as can be deduced from these lines taken from the album "Crying for Salvation":

> *Unite nationale, national integration and*
> *decentralization are a necessity.*
> *A hungry man is an angry man.*
> *A dog waiting to eat the fattest bone*
> *As his own share of the national cake*
> *May soon die of starvation.*
> *Oh my waist, oh my waist.*
> *What a hard road to travel and a very rough one.*
> *When the children of Israel began to cry for salvation*
>
> *At the bank of the red sea,*
> *It was just a matter of time.*

The above excerpt is pregnant with meaning. The first line underscores the artist's position as far as the issues of national unity, national integration and decentralization are concerned.

These three concepts, according to him, are corner-stones in the lofty project of nation building. The next line, "a hungry man is an angry man" aptly describes the feeling of the dispossessed people. Having been victims of exploitation and oppression for so long, it is only natural that they should be aggressive and hostile in their bid to free themselves from serfdom. The lines, "a dog waiting to eat the fatest bone as his own share of the national cake may soon die of starvation", alludes to the fact that Cameroonians are being nourished on the illusion that having their fair share at the "high table" is only a matter of time for them. But Afo Akom may also be saying that in spite of their very elastic capacity to endure, the waiting may be interminable. Hence, if the disaffected Cameroonians want a change towards a more democratic social and political order in their life time, then they are left with no alternative than to act now. The comparison with the children of Israel in the last lines implies that even if the struggle for a better life is long drawn or turns violent, victory is still possible.

While Tala and Afo Akom are concerned with issues of nationhood and national integration, Lapiro is worried by the chicanery and corruption of the post-colonial Cameroonian politicians. That is why he berates them in his song "Syndrome Unique":

> *Quand ils veulent arriver au pouvoir,*
> *Quand ils veulent a tout prix s'y maintenir,*
> *Ils viennent vers nous.*
> *Ils nous pompent l'air*
> *Ils nous roulent dans la farine*
> *Ils nous rappellent nos malheurs*
> *Ils nous dissent qu'ils sont la voir du Bonheur,*
> *ils sont doux,*
> *Ils sont beaux,*
> *La tchatche est belle*
> *Trop belle pours etre vraie!*
> *Tous leurs mensonges nous sont destines!*
> *Avec arguments, bien-sur!*
> *C'est nous la majorite,*
> *Le genie, la creativite, la sagesse et l'intellect...*

> *When they are seeking power,*
> *When they want to maintain their stranglehold on power,*
> *They approach us (the electorate)*
> *They boost our ego,*
> *They take us on a merry-go-round.*
> *They remind us of our poverty and misery,*
> *They tell us that they are our saviours.*
> *They are humble,*
> *They are virtuous,*
> *Their rhetoric is appealing,*
> *But, too good to be true.*
> *All their lies are directed at us,*
> *With solid arguments, of course.*
> *We constitute the majority,*
> *We represent the muse, creativity, wisdom, intellect...*

Lapiro is here following the path of the eminent Nigerian writer Chinua Achebe. They both believe that while it is necessary to point accusatory fingers at the disruption wrought by European colonialism, Nigerians and Cameroonians are not faring any better at the hands of their own people. In the above song, for example, Lapiro castigates the duplicity of post-colonial Cameroonian politicians. When they want power, they are usually exceptionally polite, affable, and even tend to wear a suave appearance. Beneath such unctuous appearance, however, lies a calculating heartlessness. They usually begin by giving the impression that they enter politics in order to help their people wheras, in reality, they enter politics in order to enrich themselves. Lapiro is in effect showing us that such concepts as moral principles and the use of power for the benefit of the people do not have any meaning to these politicians as they scramble for office. He continues his revilement:

> *Seulement, une fois au pouvoir,*
> *C'est sur nous qu'ils font la demonstration de leur force.*
> *Ils nous font la chase.*
> *Nous somme traques.*

> *La poulailler, les keufs, poudramas, babylones, les mberes...*
> *Armes de gaz lacrimogenes, de matraques, de camions a eau, de fusils automatiques.*
> *Finis la liberte!*
>
> *La seule liberte a laquelle nous avons droit est cette d'elire nos bourreaux*
> *Nous n'avons pas la liberte de manifester pacifiquement notre mecontentement.*
> *Le code penal n'aurait-il pas prevu de sanctions pour le mensonge, les fausses promesses, l'escroquerie?*
>
> *But once in positions of power, it is on us that they demonstrate their force.*
> *They chase us,*
> *They track us.*
> *The henhouse, the keufs, poudramas, babylones, mberes'*
> *armed with tear gas, batons, water canons and automatic rifles.*
> *Gone our liberty.*
> *The only liberty that is left to us is for us to elect our executioners.*
> *We do not have the liberty to demonstrate our discontent peacefully.*
> *Even though the penal code foresees sanctions for lies, false promises, fraud...*

While lapiro's disillusionment can be attributed to witnessing the adverse effects of the dishonesty of the politicians, he is also critical of the society for its cynicism and apathy. That is why he addresses the masses who are caught in a hopeless situation and are at the mercy of their leaders. He tells them directly that no one can help them but themselves:

> *Nous somme tous victimes de system pourris!*
> *Notre combat est le meme*
> *Combattre, detruire les inegalites socials!*
> *Etre respectes pas les minorites materiellement riches*
> *Est intellectuellement paumees.*
> *Avoir droit a notre part du gateau.*

> *We are all victims of the rotten system*
> *Our fight is the same.*
> *Fight to destroy social inequality,*
> *To be respected by the rich minority*
>
> *But who are intellectually impoverished,*
> *To have a right to our own share of the national cake.*

It is apparent from the above that the protest musicians whose songs have been analysed in this chapter see themselves as representing in the final analysis, the conscience of their society. That is why they criticize injustices in their society, and subject those in positions of power to relentless attack and insult in the hope that through their criticisms, they can direct their society in the path that it should be heading. They are convinced that despite the disruptive impact of European colonialism on the country, the post-colonial Cameroonian politicians and administrators must carry the bulk of the blame for the misrule and abuses which have become the trade mark of our country today. Thus, the songs go beyond a mere catalogue of gratuitous insults to become lethal weapons of political activism.

The proposals and recommendations made by the protest musicians for resolving the social, economic, and political problems which are bedeviling their country are pragmatic and feasible. Nevertheless, they are neither exhaustive nor universal. Nevertheless, they constitute a major step in the right direction.

It is important to note here that the efforts of the protest musicians are yielding palpable fruits. The marginalized Cameroonians are becoming politically aware and, as a result, are becoming more vocal in their quest for freedom of expression which they cherish as a right and as a necessary condition for good governance. The government, on its part, is beginning to listen to the pleas of the people. For example, it is taking concrete steps to improve on the Electoral Code and has introduced a Biometric system of voter registration. It is sanitizing the political process and is opening up to the fragmented opposition parties. It has embarked on vast development projects in a bid to stem growing unemployment, increase the energy potential of the country, and transform Cameroon into an emerging country in 2035. Above all, it is giving priority to youths, women, and other minority groups. It is obvious from the above that so much is being done. Of course, so much still remains to be done.

GENERAL CONCLUSION

Before a seed germinates it must first decay. A mango tree grows out of a decaying mango seed. A new Africa may be germinating in the decay of the present one – and the ancestors are presiding over the process (Mazrui, 21).

In the foregoing chapters, I have primarily attempted to address myself to the complex problems of power and marginality, particularly as they affect good governance in Cameroon and as they are reflected in some genres of contemporary Cameroonian orature with particular emphasis on popular songs/protest music. In other words, I have attempted to unravel and bring to the forefront the tense relationship that exists between the socially engaged musicians as poets of the people from the people, and members of the privileged class in power in the coutry. The intention has been to highlight what the protest musicians see as fundamental issues of national concern, and what they propose as solutions to the widening gulf between the minority who hold power and the majority who have been distanced from power.

I made the point that since the attainment of political independence, an extensive and vibrant popular/protest music culture has flourished in Cameroon. I went on to say that the songs are used to examine fundamental issues of national concern, and to criticize the political leadership. Above all, they are used to educate the marginalized people about the socio-economic quagmire and widespread malaise in the country in the belief that if the people are well informed about the causes of their predicament, they can eliminate them and work towards the creation of a common destiny.

I explained that from the nineties, the situation in the country degenerated because of the worsening economic crisis and the problems of putting in place of a competitive party system as the motor of leadership alternation in politics. These, in turn, made the relationship between the protest musicians and political power increasingly tense. The issues of governance occupied centre stage and became a bone of contention between the two opposing forces. The sprited candour with which issues of marginalization are treated in the songs emphasized the fact that as far as the artists are concerned, no matter how much power and authority a political figure may have, he is not above criticism and insult.

Among other concerns, these musicians focused on the crises of nationhood, the failure of leadership, the utopian possibilities of national development, the frenetic pursuit of wealth, the breakdown of morality, and other obstacles to self realization in a corrupt environment. They attributed these and other ills to political mismanagement, hypocrisy, collusion with the erstwhile colonial masters, dependency on foreign capital, the heavy debt burden, privatization of public enterprises, subjection to alien cultural models, and the eclipse of the traditional ways of life.

The socially engaged musicians are particularly irked and flabbergasted by the wanton greed and unbridled desires for riches which have pervaded every facet of life in the country and reduced members of the privileged class who occupy the highest echelons of the country to serving as "local black masks to much more powerful, inaccessible white faces." The protest musicians conceded that Cameroon, like other developing countries, needed to develop and modernize despite the costs. What they question is "how such development occurs, where it originates, by whom it is managed, and to whose benefits" (Gagiano, 13). The answers to these questions are crucial because most Western development experts in Cameroon for example, tend to play down the inextricable link between culture and development. As Kwesi Prah (2007:46) argues,

> *Development is impossible if it is not premised on our own historic cultural conditions. No society in the history of mankind has ever been able to progress socially on the basis of unrestrictedly borrowed cultures. An awakened Africa cannot be built on a bankrupt culture. We need to rehabilitate our culture as*

part of the national transformational process in which post-colonial Africa is immersed.

There is no doubt that the protest musicians have touched on the main reason why, in spite of the efforts and financial resources invested in development projects in Cameroon, the results have been far below expectations. Thus, if the situation is to change for the better, both Cameroonian development planners and their foreign partners must understand and recognize the role of indigenous knowledge in development programmes. This fact has been corroborated by Campton (308) when he asserted that:

> *The general lack of perpective regarding prospects for development based on culture has resulted in too much attention on finding ways and means of doing things for people rather than with them or helping them to do things for themselves. The complementary emphasis is that we desperately need to turn our attention to participatory approaches to development, to obtaining and facilitating the involvement of local people in activities designed by them to achieve their own ends. To be able to do so means a prior understanding and appreciation of indigenous culture by planners and workers.*

Both Prah and Campton support my main contention in this book which, put quite simply, is that orature is of vital importance to national development, national identity, and national integration. I also made the point that since history has a tendency of repeating itself, there is an urgent need for us to retrace our steps and go back to our culture in general and our orature in particular. A return to our orature will definitely enable us to negotiate a better future by avoiding the repetition of the mistakes of the past. I have also emphasized the need to see issues whether developmental, educational, or political from Cameroonian perspectives. I can only add here that as Cameroonians, we need to take the following recommendations of Okoh (246), more seriously.

> *There is a common tendency to view 'development' as synonymous with technological or scientific advances even improved, higher standards of living in a society... We hear everywhere and every day so much talk about*

'development'. In most cases the expression is preceded by such tags as 'national', 'economic', 'cultural', 'political', even 'democratic'. We posit first and foremost, then, that development is not necessarily to be equated with technological progress or advancement in the field of science. More importantly, we contend here that if we are to achieve the feat or phenomenon called development- in whatever colour, size, shape, or by any other label in addition to those above- this must begin from the mind. And for the mind to become developed, it must be occupied by positive values. And for us as a nation to imbibe positive cultural values, we need to look inwards or more specifically, understand, then explore the very strength and resources of our oral literature.

Thus, the difficulty that is facing us as Cameroonians at the present juncture, is how to rediscover our own identity. We can resolve that difficulty by rehabilitating our culture and by reorientating our curricula in order to transform our development into a human-centred process with the objective of improving our welfare.

As concerns the crises of nationhood, the populist musicians argued that it cannot be resolved politically because the hegemonic party system in place cannot guarantee power alternation at regular intervals in the country. Furthermore, the country's parliament is not playing its pivotal role as the principal forum for political debates. Consequently, it cannot provide political direction to the country. Cameroon, like most African countries, lacks a responsible opposition and a vigorous civil society. In fact, the opposition parties are so fragmented that it is almost impossible for them to enter into voluntary fusion. The media is, to say the least, a toothless bulldog. Finally, the intelligentsia has abdicated its historic responsibility. Thus, in the light of the above, the musicians perceive themselves and are perceived by their fellow Cameroonians as the only pro-democracy agency capable of fighting for genuine democracy and giving a sense of direction to Cameroon.

It is important to note that the protest musicians neither call for violence nor advocate a revolutionary overthrow of the regime in place. Rather they recommend a gradualist approach to change and for a peaceful return to honourable ideals as those of hard work, responsibility, accountability, freedom, justice, respect for one another, and the communion of persons on which our traditional societies were founded.

One social scourge on which the socially engaged musicians have harped over and over again is corruption because of its disastrous consequences on the marginalized segment of the population. Corruption, as I explained in Chapter Three, is the abuse of the power entrusted to us for our personal gain. It is a worldwide phenomenon in the sense that there is no region in the world that is entirely free from it. Nevertheless, it is a matter of great concern for Cameroon because a few years ago, the country was rated on the Transparency International's Corruption Perceptions Index as the most corrupt country in the world. Since then however, the Cameroon Government has put in place stringent measures to fight the scourge. That has led to the arrest and imprisonment of several senior members of the ruling elite who covet unearned luxuries while the majority of their fellow countrymen are mired in hopeless poverty. The fight against the scourge continues but the efforts are constantly being foiled by greed and by the pressure to survive in a competitive world.

This book, therefore, is a plea for a recentering of Cameroonian realities. Thus, if the issues of power and marginality in the country are to be addressed more successfully than heretofore, and if the politically fraught conditions of Cameroon are to be ameliorated then, we must, as Cameroonians be prepared to undergo a radical change of mentality. We must be ready to rehabilitate our orature and press it into service to raise the level of consciousness in the society in order to provoke positive change. Finally, we must be able to recognize our protest musicians especially in their roles as social critics which are reminiscent of the positive heroes of our myths and legends.

It is important to note the similarities between positive heroes and the protest musicians. Both have not, to use Fonlon's expression "garnered gold; they have sought salutary knowledge, they are strangers to ignoble strife; it is in grief that they grew strong". They are both scarce in society, and where they happen to exist, they find it difficult to operate. Finally, their fate is the same. That is, they all pass through the same sequence of "temporary acceptance, growing opposition, rejection, suffering, dereliction, vindication". The fact that they are vindicated in the end is an indication that their mission will eventually triumph over the forces of human tyranny.

BIBLIOGRAPHY

Abrahams, Roger D. 1983. *African Folktales.* New York: Pantheon Book.

Achebe, Chinua. 1958. *Things Fall Apart.* London: Henemann.

___. 1987. *Anthills of the Savannah,* Lagos, Nigeria: Heinemann Educational Books Ltd.

___. 1975. *Morning Yet on Creation Day.* London: Heinemann.

Adedeji, Adebayo ed. 1993. *Africa Within the World: Beyond Dispossession and Independence.* London: Zed Books.

Agbase, J. B. 2000. *"The Place of Yoruba Proverbs in the understanding of Yoruba Philosophy and Education".* http://www.siue.edu/-mofola/journal, 6/12/2009.

Agbor, Ambang, A. A. and Ojong Enorfor E. 2010. *Democracy and Power Alteration in Africa: A Dialectic Analysis of the Political Watersheds of an Emerging Africa.* Yaounde: African Publications.

Agovi, K. 1995. *"Theatre, Law and Order in Pre-Colonial Africa",* in Theatre and politics in Africa, UCLA: Department of Film and Theatre.

Ako, Edward. 1996. *"Children's Literature in Cameroon",* in A Review Essay. Pp 310 – 317.

Alembong, Nol. 2010. *Cameroon's Western Grassland Incantations Background, Society, Cosmology.* Gottingen, Germany: Cuvillier publishing House.

___. 2011. *Standpoints on African Orature.* Yaounde: Presses Universiteures de Yaounde.

Ambanasom, A. Shadrach. 2003. E*ducation of the Deprived: A Study of Four Cameroonian Playwrights.* Yaounde: Presses Universitaires de Yaounde.

Arewa, Ojo and Alan Dundes. 1964. *Proverbs and the Ethnography of Speaking Folklore.* Massachusetts, U.S.A: Warner Modular Publications, Inc.

Bascon, William. 1953. *"Folklore and Anthropology".* Journal of American Folklore 66, 283 – 290.

Biernaczky, S. 1984. *Folklore in Africa Today.* Budapest: African Research Project.

Bjornson, Richard. 1991. *The African Quest for Freedom and Identity.* Bloomington, Indiana: Indiana University Press.

Brumfit, C. J. and R. A Carter. Eds. 1986. *Literature and Language Teaching.* Oxford: Oxford University Press.

Bruvand, Jan Harold. 1978. *The Study of American Folklore: An Introduction.* New York: W.W. Norton and Company, Inc.

Buckley, W. 1967. *Sociology and Modern Systems Theory.* Englewood Cliffs, N. J: Prentice Hall.

Bukenya, Austin et al. 1994. *Understanding Oral Literature.* Nairobi: University of Nairobi Press.

Busch, Gary, K. 2011. *Consensual Rape in the Franceafrique Currency Market.* Memeograph.

Cabral, A. 1973. *Return to the Source: Selected Speeches of Amilcar Cabral.* Ed. Africa Information Service. New York: Monthly Review.

Campton, J. L. 1980. *"Indigenous Folk Media in Rural Development". In Indigenous Knowledge Systems and Development.* Eds. Brokensha, et al. Lanham: University Press of America. Pp 307 – 319.

Chinweizu, et al. 1983. *Towards the Decolonisation of African Literature.* Enugu, Nigeria: Fourth Dimension Publishing.

Chukwuma, H. O 1981. *Oral Tale.* Denmark: Dangaroo press.

Conrad, Joseph. 1963. *Nostromo.* London: Dent.

Coser, A. L. and B. Rosenberg. eds. 1969. *Sociological Theory: A Book of readings.* London: MacMillan Company.

Courlander, Harold. 1975. *A Treasury of African Folklore.* New York: Crown Publishers, Inc.

Dasylva, A. O. 1999. *Classificatory Paradigms in African Oral Narratives.* Ibadan Cultural Studies Group.

Duerden, Dennis and Cosmo Pieterse. 1975. *African Writers Talking.* London: Heinemann.

Dze-Ngwa, Willibroad. 2008. *"National Unity and National Integration, 1961 – 2000: Dreams and Realities."* Ph.D Thesis, Department of History, University of Yaounde I.

Fadipe, N. A. 1970. *The Sociology of the Yoruba* Ibadan: Ibadan University Press.

Fanon, Frantz. 1963. *The Wretched of the Earth.* New York: Grove Press.

Finnegan, Ruth. 1970. *Oral Literature in Africa.* Oxford: The Clarendon Press.

Fonlon, Bernard. 1959. *To Every African Freshman or The Nature, End and Purpose of University Studies.* Victoria, West Cameroon: 1969.

Fonlon, Bernard. ed. 1965. *ABBIA: Cameroon Cultural review.* Yaounde: Edition CLE.

Freire, Paulo. 1982. *Pedagogy of the Oppressed.* New York: Continuum Publishing Corporation.

Furniss, Grahan. and Liz Gunner. 1995. *Power, Marginality and African Oral Literature.* Cambridge: Cambridge University Press.

Gagiano, Annie. 2000. *Achebe, Head, Marechera: On Power And Change in Africa.* London: Lynne Runner Publishers, Inc.

Greene, Robert. 2000. *The 48 Laws of Power.* London: Penguin Books Ltd.

Grugeon, Elizabeth and Peter Walsden. Eds. 1978. *Literature and Learning.* London: Ward Lock Educational.

Gugelberger, Georg. 1985. *Marxism and African Literature.* London: John Currey Ltd.

Imam, Alhaji Abubakar. 1966. *Magana Jari Ce.* Zaria, Nigeria: Northern Nigerian Publishing Company.

Jackson, Bruce. 1987. *Fieldwork .* Chicago, U.S.A: University of Illinois Press.

Kaschula, Russell. 2001. *African Oral Literature: Functions in Contemporary Society.* Claremont, 7735 South Africa: New Africa Books (Pty) Ltd.

Kelso, J. A. ed. 1971. *Proverbs in Encyclopedia of religion and Ethics.* Vol. 10. New York: Tand T. Clark.

Leaming, David Adams. 1998. *Mythology: The Voyage of the Hero.* Oxford. Oxford University Press.
Limon, E. S. 1985. *"Western Marxism and Folklore: A critical Introduction."* In *Journal of American Folklore*, 9, 379 – 382, pp 45 – 6.
Lindfors, Bernth. ed. 1977. *Forms of Folklore in Africa.* Austin, Texas: University of Texas Press.
Mazrui, Ali. 1986. *The Africans: A Triple Heritage.* Toronto, Canada: Little, Brown and Company.
Mbangwana, Paul Nkad. 1993. *"Cameroon oral tale in Ngemba: A Study in Language and Social Setting".* Doctorat D'Etat Thesis, University of Yaounde.
Mokwunye, E. 1978. *Cultural Activities in Nigerian Schools.* Ibadan, Nigeria: Oxford University Press.
Murfin, Ross and Supryia Ray. 1998. *The Bedford Glossary of Critical and Literary Terms.* Boston: Bedford.
Nanda, S. and R. L Warms. 1998. *Cultural Anthropology.* Belmont: Wardsworth.
Ngam Gilead Nkwain. (2010). *"The Relevance of Folklore in Development: The Case of Oral Tales of the Cameroonian Grassfields."* Ph.D Thesis, Department of African Literature and Civilization, University of Yaounde I.
Ngara, Emmanuel. 1985. *Art and Ideology in the African Novel.* London: Heinemann.
Ngarka, Tala et al. eds. 2008. *Lapai Journal of Humanities.* Vol. 2, N°. 1.
Ngeh, Andrew Tata. 2011. *"Aesthetic Paradigms of Critical and Socialist Realisms in the Cameroon poetry of English Expression".* Ph.D Thesis, Department of African Literature and Civilization, University of Yaounde I.
Ngoh, Victor Julius. 2004. *Cameroon from a Federal to a Unitary State (1961 – 1972): A Critical Study.* Limbe, Cameroon: Design House.
Nguefak, Adeline epouse Kamdem. 2009. *"La Chanson Populaire Contemporaire comme forme de Resistance: Le cas du Cameroun".* Doctorat (Ph.D)

Thesis," Department of African Literature and Civilization, University of Yaounde I.
Ngugi, wa Thiong'o. 1977. *Writers in Politics: A Re-Engagement with issues of Literature and Society.* Oxford: Heneimann.
Nnolim, Charles. 200. *Literature, the Arts, and Cultural Development.* Port Harcourt, Nigeria: Pam Unique Publishers.
Nyamnjoh, B. F. and Jude Fokwang. 2005. *Entertaining Repression: Music and Politics in Post-Colonial Cameroon.* Oxford: Oxford University Press.
Nyamnjoh, Francis. 1999. *"Cameroon: A Country United by Ethnic Ambition and difference".* African Affairs, 98, 101 – 118.
Ojinmah, Umelo. 1991. *Chinua Achebe: New Perspectives.* Ibadan, Nigerai: Spectrum Books Ltd.
Okoh, Nkem. 2008. *Preface to Oral Literature.* Onitsha, Nigeria: Africana First Publishers.
Okpewho, Isidore. 2000. *"African Mythology and Africa's Political Impasse"* Research in African Literature, 29, 1, 8.
__ __ __. 1985. *The Heritage of African Poetry.* Essex, England: Longman Group Ltd.
__ __ __. 1990. *The Oral Perspective in Africa.* Ibadan, Nigeria: Spectrum Books Limited.
Olaniyam, Tejumola, and Ato Quayson. 2008. *African Literature: An Anthology of Criticism and History. Oxford*: Blackwell.
Olaniyan, Richard. ed. 1982. *African History and Culture.* Ikeja, Lagos, Nigeria: Longman Nigerian Limited.
Ong, J. Walter. 1989. *Orality and Literature,* London: Routledge.
Ongoum, L. M. and I. C. Tcheho. 1989. *Oral Literature in Africa Today: Theoretical and Practical Approaches.* Proceedings of the International Symposium, Yaounde: University of Yaounde.
Opata, Damian et al. 2000. *Major Themes in African Literature.* Nsukka, Nigeria: AP Express Publishers.

Penjore, Dorji. 2006. *"Folktales and Education: The Role of Bhutanese Folktales in Value Transmission."* http://www.grossnationalhappi, 02/02/2010

Piaget, J. 1970. *Structuralism.* New York: Basic Books Inc.

Prah, Kwesi. 2007. *"Indigenous Knowledge Systems and the African Development":* The Political Roles of Oral Genres with Specific References to Zulu (South Africa) and Goun (Benin), by M. V. Zounmenou, www.wisdom-tales.com/programs, 16/09/2008.

Priebe, K. Richard. 1988. *Myth, Realism, and the West African Writer.* Trenton, New Jersey: African World Press.

Roberts, V. Edgar, and Henry E. Jacobs. 2000. eds. *Literature: An Introduction to Reading and writing.* New Jersey: Upper Saddle River.

Rosenberg, Donna. 1996. *folklore, Myths and Legends: A World Perspective.* Lincolnwood: NTC Publishing Group.

Said, Edward. 1978. *Orientalism.* New York: Routeledge.

___. 1994. *Culture and Imperialism.* London: Vintage.

Sandstorm, Kent, et al. 2003. *Symbols, Selves, and Social Reality.* Los Angeles, California: Roxbury Publishing Company.

Seitel, Peter. 1980. *See So That We May See: Performances and Interpretations of Traditional Tales from Tanzania.* Bloomington: Indiana University Press.

Sharrock, W. W. 2003. *Understanding Modern Sociology.* London: Sage Publications.

Simms, Norman. ed. 1982. *Oral and Traditional Literatures.* Hamilton, New Zealand: Outrigger Publishers.

Skinner, Neil 1977. *Anthropology of Hausa Literature in Translation.* Madison, Wisconsin: The University of Wisconsin Press.

Street, J. 2001. *"Rock, Pop and Politics"* in *S. Firth et al.* eds. *Pop and Rock.* Cambridge: Cambridge University Press.

Tabuwe, Aletum, and Fisiy Fonyuy. 1989. *Socio-Political Integration and the Nso Institutions.* Yaounde, Cameroon: SOPECAM.

Tala, Kashim Ibrahim and Henry K. Jick. 2008. *"Lapiro de Mbanga and Political Vision in Contemporary Cameroon"* in Lapai Journal of humanities. Vol. 2. N°. 1.

Tala, Kashim Ibrahim. 1984. *An Introduction to Cameroon Oral Literature.* Yaounde: The University of Yoaunde press.Tala, Kashim Ibrahim. 1999. *Orature in Africa.* Saskatchewan, Canada: University of Saskatchewan Press.

Thompson, Stith. 1977. *The Folktale.* Berkeley: University of California Press.

Turner, Victor. 1967. *The Forest of Symbols: Aspects of Ndembu Rituals.* Ithaca: Cornell University Press.

Vakunta, Peter. 2010. *"Lapiroisms: Language of Resistance in Cameroonian Music".* http://www.postnewsline.com/2010/11/lapiroisms-language-of-resistance-in-cameroonian-music."

Vazquez, Adolfo Sanchez. 1973 in *"Art and Society: Essays in Marxist Aesthetics," transl. by Mario Riofrancos*, Monthly review Press. 9. 84.

Wellek, Rene. 1986. *A History of Modern Criticism 1750 – 1950.* New Haven and London: Yale University Press.

www.ingramcontent.com/pod-product-compliance
Lightning Source LLC
Chambersburg PA
CBHW021827300426
44114CB00009BA/359